"Most can raise the flowers now,
For all have got the seed."

—TENNYSON

# A TESTAMENT

BRAMHALL HOUSE    NEW YORK

# FRANK LLOYD WRIGHT

This edition is published by Bramhall House,
a division of Clarkson N. Potter, Inc.,
by arrangement with the original publisher,
Horizon Press, Inc.


(G)

# CONTENTS

INDEX TO ILLUSTRATIONS  page 7

## BOOK ONE—AUTOBIOGRAPHICAL

**PART ONE**  ARCHITECTURE IS ALWAYS HERE AND NOW  page 17  THE SEED 17  THE CONFUSION 20  AWAKENING 23  REALIZATION 24  RETROGRESSION 24  "THE CHICAGO SCHOOL" 33  DISASTER 36  CONTRIBUTION 37  MAN AND THE MACHINE 37  THE FIELD 39  CIVILIZATION AS ABSTRACTION 58  POET—"UNACKNOWLEDGED LEGISLATOR OF THE WORLD" 59  CONFORMITY 60  NEW THOUGHT 61  ROMANCE—THE FREE PHILOSOPHY 62  JEFFERSON'S ARISTOI 62  INTEGRITY 63  NEW OR OLD 81  NAISSANCE 81  REVERSION 82  THE VIEW 82  BETRAYAL 83  FAITH IN MAN 84  THE TROJAN HORSE—CONFIDENTIAL 84  CONSEQUENCES 86  THE EXPEDIENT 87  THE SUBSTITUTE 88  "THE COMMON MAN" 97  THE NEED FOR THE NEW AMERICAN 98  MAN ABOVE LAW OR LAW ABOVE MAN 99  WALT WHITMAN—SEER OF DEMOCRACY 99  BEGINNING 100  INSIDE OUT—OUTSIDE IN 102

**PART TWO**  FORM—A BIRTH 105  NEW PHILOSOPHY 106  NEW INTEGRITY 106  PRINCIPLE BEFORE PRECEDENT 107  "NORMALCY" 108  THE NATURE OF NATURE 109

NOW—FREEDOM IS FROM WITHIN 112    THE EUROPEAN CONTRADICTION 130    DISCOVERY 131    INCIDENTAL 133    ORNAMENT 133    INTEGRATION INTRINSIC 134 THE IDEA 135    STANDARDIZED 136

PART THREE    CONCERNING THE THIRD DIMENSION 155    ORGANIC ORNAMENT 157    ROMANCE 158    THE CRITIC 159 USONIA 160    SCIENCE AND THE SCIENTIST 160    THE SUBSTITUTE 177    THE MONUMENTAL 178    SELF-POSSESSION 179    DEMOCRACY 180    THE APPEAL 180    FREEDOM 181    TRADITION 181

PART FOUR    THE CITY 185    IDEAS AND IDEALS 186    YOUTH AND ARCHITECTURE 187    RETROSPECT 189    TECHNOLOGY AGAIN 191    SALVATION 192    ORGANIC CHARACTER-ISTICS 202    THE NEW CLICHE 203    INFLUENCES AND INFERENCES 205    WISDOM 207

# BOOK TWO—THE NEW ARCHITECTURE

PART ONE
PRINCIPLES    I. THE EARTH LINE 219    THE MODULAR OF THE KINDER-GARTEN TABLE 220    II. IMPULSE TO GROW 221    III. CHARACTER IS A NATURAL 222    IV. TENUITY PLUS CON-TINUITY 223    V. THE THIRD DIMENSION: INTERPRETA-TION 224    VI. SPACE 225    VII. FORM 226    ORGANIC UNIT 227    VIII. SHELTER: INHERENT HUMAN FACTOR 227    THE CLIENT 228    IX. MATERIALS 229    STYLE 229    OWNERSHIP 229    WHAT IS NATURAL 230 ADDENDUM I 231    FURNITURE 231    THE CAMERA EYE 232    THE PROFESSION 249    THEY ALSO SERVE 250

PART TWO    HUMANITY—THE LIGHT OF THE WORLD 253    AMERICAN GENIUS 255

PHOTOGRAPHERS' CREDITS 256

# INDEX TO ILLUSTRATIONS

ADELMAN LAUNDRY, MILWAUKEE,
WISCONSIN, 1948, PROJECT
page 176   DRAWING
      176   SECTION
AMERICAN SYSTEM READY-CUT
DUPLEX FLATS, 1915, PROJECT
      122   DRAWING
      122   PLANS
ARIZONA STATE CAPITOL, "OASIS,"
PHOENIX, ARIZONA, 1957, PROJECT
      236   AERIAL PERSPECTIVE
      237   PLAN
      237   SECTION
BANFF PAVILION, ALBERTA, CANADA,
1911
      80   DRAWING
BARNSDALL ("HOLLYHOCK") HOUSE,
OLIVE HILL, LOS ANGELES,
CALIFORNIA, 1917-20
      137   SIDE VIEW
      137   PLAN
      137   EXTERIOR
BETH SHOLEM SYNAGOGUE,
PHILADELPHIA, PENNSYLVANIA, 1954
      210   DRAWING
      211   SECTION

      212   DRAWING, NIGHT VIEW
      213   PLANS
BOCK ATELIERS, 1902
      46   DRAWING
      46   PLAN
BOOTH HOUSE, GLENCOE, ILLINOIS,
1911, PROJECT
      94   DRAWING
      94   PLAN
      95   PLAN
      95   DRAWING OF BRIDGE
CHENEY HOUSE, OAK PARK,
ILLINOIS, 1904
      52   FIRST SKETCH
      52   PLAN
      52   DRAWING
CHRISTIAN SCIENCE CHURCH,
BOLINAS, MARIN COUNTY,
CALIFORNIA, 1957
      233   DRAWING
      233   PLAN
CITY NATIONAL BANK BUILDING
AND HOTEL, MASON CITY, IOWA,
1909
      92   DRAWING
      92   PLAN

CLUB HOUSE, DELAVAN LAKE,
WISCONSIN, 1902, PROJECT

    65   DRAWING

COONLEY HOUSE, RIVERSIDE,
ILLINOIS, 1908

    68   DRAWING

    69   PLAN

    69   EXTERIOR

    70   EXTERIOR

    71   LIVING ROOM

    72   SKETCH FOR COONLEY PLAYHOUSE WINDOW (1912)

    72   COURTYARD

    73   SKETCH FOR STABLE WINDOW

    73   DRAWING OF CEILING SCREEN

CUTTEN HOUSE, DOWNER'S GROVE,
ILLINOIS, 1912, PROJECT

    96   DRAWING

    96   PLAN

DRAWING, 1888

    25   SHOWN TO LOUIS SULLIVAN BY FRANK LLOYD WRIGHT ON APPLYING FOR JOB

ENNIS HOUSE, LOS ANGELES,
CALIFORNIA, 1922-24

    148   DRAWING

    149   EXTERIOR

    149   PLAN

FIRST UNITARIAN CHURCH,
MADISON, WISCONSIN, 1949

    174   SECTION OF ROOF

    174   DRAWING

    175   EXTERIOR

FLORIDA SOUTHERN COLLEGE,
LAKELAND, FLORIDA, MUSIC
BUILDING, 1957

    234   DRAWING

    234   PLAN

    235   PLAN OF BALCONY AND ELEVATION

FLORIDA SOUTHERN COLLEGE,
LAKELAND, FLORIDA, ANN PFEIFFER
CHAPEL, 1940

    168   PLAN

    168   EXTERIOR

    169   SECTION

FREEMAN HOUSE, LOS ANGELES,
CALIFORNIA, 1924

    150   DRAWING

    151   DRAWING

    151   PLANS

JIYU GAKUEN SCHOOL, TOKYO,
JAPAN, 1921

    128   DRAWING

GALE HOUSE, OAK PARK, ILLINOIS, 1909

    74   DRAWING

    74   PLANS

    75   EXTERIOR

GLADNEY HOUSE, FORT WORTH,
TEXAS, 1925, PROJECT

    161   DRAWING

GREEK ORTHODOX CHURCH,
MILWAUKEE, WISCONSIN, 1956,
PROJECT

    216   DRAWING

    216   PLAN

SOLOMON R. GUGGENHEIM MUSEUM,
NEW YORK CITY, 1943

    169   DRAWING

HARDY HOUSE, RACINE, WISCONSIN,
1905

    54   DRAWING

    54   EXTERIOR

    54   PLANS

    55   DRAWING

HEATH HOUSE, BUFFALO, NEW YORK,
1905

    56   EXTERIOR

56 PLANS

56 EXTERIOR

**HEURTLEY HOUSE, OAK PARK,
ILLINOIS, 1902**

47 EXTERIOR

47 PLANS

**HILLSIDE HOME SCHOOL,
SPRING GREEN, WISCONSIN, 1902**

44 DRAWING

45 EXTERIOR

45 PLAN

**IMPERIAL HOTEL, TOKYO, JAPAN,
1915-22**

123 PRELIMINARY STUDY

124 EXTERIOR

124 CONSTRUCTION DETAILS

125 EMPEROR'S ENTRANCE

126 GARDEN COURT

127 BANQUET HALL

127 BALLROOM

**S. C. JOHNSON AND SON, INC.
ADMINISTRATION BUILDING,
RACINE, WISCONSIN, 1936-39**

170 PLAN

171 INTERIOR

**S. C. JOHNSON AND SON RESEARCH
CENTER, RACINE, WISCONSIN, 1947**

172 EXTERIOR

173 SECTION

**KAUFMANN HOUSE, "FALLING-
WATER," BEAR RUN, PENNSYLVANIA,
1936**

165 EXTERIOR

165 SECTION

**LADIES' HOME JOURNAL HOUSE,
1900, PROJECT**

41 DRAWING

41 PLANS

**LARKIN BUILDING, BUFFALO,
NEW YORK, 1904**

48 DRAWING

48 PLAN

49 EXTERIOR

50 EXTERIOR

51 INTERIOR

**LEXINGTON TERRACE, CHICAGO,
ILLINOIS, 1909, PROJECT**

89 DRAWING, DETAIL

89 DRAWING, INNER COURT

90 DRAWING, PERSPECTIVE

91 PLAN

**LUXFER PRISM FACADE, CHICAGO,
ILLINOIS, 1897**

30 DRAWING

**MARTIN HOUSE, BUFFALO,
NEW YORK, 1904**

53 EXTERIOR

53 PLAN

**MIDWAY GARDENS, CHICAGO,
ILLINOIS, 1913-14**

114 DRAWING, PERSPECTIVE

114 SECTION AND ELEVATION

115 SECTIONS

116 ELEVATION

116 EXTERIOR

117 DRAWING, INTERIOR

118 EXTERIOR

119 DESIGN FOR ORNAMENT

120 OPEN GARDENS

121 DESIGN FOR ORNAMENT

**THE MILE-HIGH ILLINOIS, CHICAGO,
ILLINOIS, 1956, PROJECT**

238 PRELIMINARY SKETCH

Foldout
between
pages

240-249 TAPROOT FOUNDATION
PLANS: BASE, 320th, 528th FLOORS
TYPICAL ELEVATION, SECTION
PERSPECTIVE
SIDE, REAR AND FRONT ELEVATIONS

MILLARD HOUSE ("LA MINIATURA"),
PASADENA, CALIFORNIA, 1921-23
    144   DRAWING
    145   EXTERIOR
    145   PLANS

MONONA TERRACE PROJECT,
MADISON, WISCONSIN, 1955
    209   DRAWING
    209   PLANS

MOTION PICTURE THEATRE,
1897, PROJECT
    32   DRAWING

NAKOMA COUNTRY CLUB, MADISON,
WISCONSIN, 1924, PROJECT
    152   DRAWING
    152   SECTION THROUGH WIGWAM
    152   PLAN

NOBLE APARTMENT HOUSE,
LOS ANGELES, CALIFORNIA, 1929,
PROJECT
    164   DRAWING
    164   SECTION
    164   PLANS

ODAWARA HOTEL, NAGOYA, JAPAN,
1917, PROJECT
    128   DRAWING

HAROLD C. PRICE HOUSE,
PHOENIX, ARIZONA, 1955
    198   EXTERIOR
    198   PLAN
    199   ATRIUM
    200   LIVING ROOM

HAROLD C. PRICE, JR. HOUSE,
BARTLESVILLE, OKLAHOMA, 1955
    193   EXTERIOR
    194   LIVING ROOM
    194   PLANS
    195   MASTER BEDROOM
    195   EXTERIOR

H. C. PRICE COMPANY TOWER,
BARTLESVILLE, OKLAHOMA, 1953-56
    196   DRAWING
    197   EXTERIOR

ROBIE HOUSE, CHICAGO, ILLINOIS, 1909
    76   DRAWING
    76   PLANS
    77   EXTERIOR
    78   EXTERIOR
    78   LIVING ROOM
    78   DETAIL, WINDOW PATTERN
    79   DETAIL, ENTRY BELOW

"ROMEO AND JULIET" WINDMILL,
HILLSIDE, SPRING GREEN,
WISCONSIN, 1896
    31   EXTERIOR
    31   SECTION

ROSENBAUM HOUSE, FLORENCE,
ALABAMA, 1939
    167   EXTERIOR
    167   PLAN
    167   EXTERIOR

SCHOOLHOUSE FOR NEGRO
CHILDREN, ROSENWALD FOUNDA-
TION, LA JOLLA, CALIFORNIA, 1928
    163   DRAWING

SMALL TOWN HOUSE, 1912, PROJECT
    113   DRAWING

SPORTS PAVILION, NEW YORK,
1956, PROJECT
    214   DRAWING
    215   PLAN OF GRANDSTAND
    215   SECTION

STORER HOUSE, LOS ANGELES,
CALIFORNIA, 1922-23
    146   DRAWING
    147   EXTERIOR
    147   PLANS

STUDIO FOR THE ARCHITECT,
FLORENCE, ITALY, 1910, PROJECT

    93   DRAWING

STUDY FOR BRICK AND CONCRETE,
BUILDING, 1904

    43   DRAWING

TAHOE SUMMER COLONY, EMERALD
BAY, LAKE TAHOE, CALIFORNIA,
1922, PROJECT

    138   BARGE, FAMILY TYPE, DRAWING
           AND PLAN

    138   PLAN OF COLONY

    139   CABIN, SHORE TYPE, DRAWING
           AND PLAN

    140   CABIN, FIR TREE TYPE, DRAWING
           AND PLAN

    141   BARGE, "FALLEN LEAF," DRAWING
           AND PLAN

    141   BARGE FOR TWO, DRAWING AND
           PLAN

    142   CABIN, WIGWAM TYPE, DRAWING
           AND PLAN

    143   CABIN, LODGE TYPE, DRAWING
           AND PLAN

TALIESIN III, SPRING GREEN,
WISCONSIN, 1925

    162   EXTERIOR

    162   ARCHITECT'S STUDY

TALIESIN WEST, PARADISE VALLEY
NEAR PHOENIX, ARIZONA, 1938

    166   EXTERIOR

    166   INTERIOR

UNITY TEMPLE, OAK PARK,
ILLINOIS, 1906

    66   DRAWING AND PLAN

    67   EXTERIOR

WINSLOW HOUSE, RIVER FOREST,
ILLINOIS, 1893

    26   DRAWING AND PLAN

    27   EXTERIOR

FRANK LLOYD WRIGHT

    FRONTISPIECE

FRANK LLOYD WRIGHT STUDIO,
OAK PARK, ILLINOIS, 1895

    28   EXTERIOR

    28   OUTER OFFICE

    29   DRAUGHTING ROOM

    29   PLAN

YAHARA BOAT HOUSE, MADISON,
WISCONSIN, 1902

    42   DRAWING AND PLAN

# BOOK ONE
## AUTOBIOGRAPHICAL

PART ONE

Philosophy is to the mind of the architect as eyesight to his steps. The term "genius" when applied to him simply means a man who understands what others only know about. A poet, artist or architect, necessarily "understands" in this sense and is likely, if not careful, to have the term "genius" applied to him; in which case he will no longer be thought human, trustworthy or companionable.

Whatever may be his medium of expression he utters truth with manifest beauty of thought. If he is an architect, his buildings are natural. In him, philosophy and genius live by each other, but the combination is subject to popular suspicion and the appellation "genius" likely to settle him — so far as the public is concerned.

Everyone engaged in creative work is subject to persecution by the odious comparison. Odious comparisons dog the footsteps of all creation wherever the poetic principle is involved because the inferior mind learns only by comparisons; comparisons, usually equivocal, made by selfish interests each for the other. But the superior mind learns by analyses: the study of Nature.

The collected evidence of my own active work-time is for my guidance, pride and pleasure as much as for any other reason half so good. Romanticist by nature — self-confessed — I am pleased by the thread of structural consistency

I see inspiring the complete texture of the work revealed in my designs and plans, varied building for my American people over a long period of time: from the beginning — 1893 — to this time, 1957. This architecture is often called "engineering-architecture." I plead guilty to the tough impeachment.

So the poet in the engineer and the engineer in the poet and both in the architect may be seen here working together, lifelong. William Blake — poet — has said "exuberance is Beauty." It took me sometime to know just what the great Blake meant when he wrote that. For one thing, this lesson, now valuable to the creative architect, I would finally illustrate here; in this poetry-crushing, transitory era of the Machine wherein development of a national culture or even a personal culture of one's own has long been so recreant. Blake meant that Beauty always is the consequence of utter fullness of nature in expression: expression intrinsic. Excess never to be mistaken for exuberance; excess being always vulgar. He who knows the difference between excess and exuberance is aware of the nature of the poetic principle, and not likely to impoverish, or be impoverished, by his work. The more a horse is Horse, a bird Bird, the more a man is Man, a woman Woman, the better? The more a design is creative revelation of intrinsic nature, whatever the medium or form of expression, the better.

"Creative," then, implies exuberance. It is not only true expression but true interpretation, as a whole, of the significance, truth and force of Nature, raised to the fullest power by the poet. That design revealing truth of inner being most abundantly is best design. Design that lasts longest; remembered by mankind with greatest profit and pride.

Art formalized, empty of this innate significance, is the cliché: cut and dried content no longer humanely significant. The so-called modern "classic" has become cliché and does not live under this definition of exuberance. Only the mind of one who has left the region of the soul and inhabits the region of the nervous system in our time mistakes florid or senseless elaboration for exuberance. The "efficient" mind that would put Pegasus to the plough never knows the difference between the Curious and the Beautiful or the difference between the prosaic and the poetic.

# ARCHITECTURE IS ALWAYS HERE AND NOW

Victor Hugo, in the most illuminating essay on architecture yet written, declared European Renaissance "the setting sun all Europe mistook for dawn." During 500 years of elaborate reiteration of restatements by classic column, entablature and pediment — all finally became moribund. Victor Hugo, greatest modern of his time, went on to prophesy: the great mother-art, architecture, so long formalized, pictorialized by way of man's intellect could and would come spiritually alive again. In the latter days of the nineteenth or early in the twentieth century man would see architecture revive. The soul of man would by then, due to the changes wrought upon him, be awakened by his own critical necessity.

## THE SEED

I was fourteen years old when this usually expurgated chapter in *Notre Dame* profoundly affected my sense of the art I was born to live with — lifelong; architecture. His story of the tragic decline of the great mother-art never left my mind.

The University of Wisconsin had no course in architecture. As civil-engineer, therefore, several months before I was to receive a degree, I ran away from school (1888) to go to work in some real architect's office in Chicago. I did not want to be an engineer. A visit to the pawnbroker's — "old man Perry" — made exodus possible. My father's Gibbon's *Rome* and Plutarch's *Lives* (see Alcibiades) and the mink cape collar my mother had sewed to my overcoat financed the enterprise.

There, in Chicago, so many years after Victor Hugo's remarkable prophecy, I found Naissance had already begun. The sun — architecture — was rising!

As premonition, then, the pre-Raphaelites had appeared in England but they seemed sentimentalist reformers. Beside the mark. Good William Morris and John Ruskin were much in evidence in Chicago intellectual circles at the time. The Mackintoshes of Scotland; restless European protestants also — Van de Velde of Belgium, Berlage of Holland, Adolph Loos and Otto Wagner of Vienna: all were genuine protestants, but then seen and heard only in Europe. Came Van de Velde with *Art Nouveau*, himself predecessor of the subsequent Bauhaus. Later, in 1910 when I went to Germany by instigation of Professor Kuno Francke, there I found only the rebellious "Secession" in full swing. I met no architects.

But more important than all, a great protestant, grey army engineer, Dankmar Adler, builder and philosopher, together with his young partner, a genius, rebel from the Beaux-Arts of Paris, Louis H. Sullivan, were practising architecture there in Chicago, about 1887.


After tramping the Chicago streets for some days I got in with Cecil Corwin, foreman for J. L. Silsbee, then Chicago's foremost resident architect. He was a minister's son — as I was — and so were Cecil and the other four draughtsmen there at the time. One year later I was accepted by Mr. Sullivan and went to work for "Adler and Sullivan" then the only moderns in architecture, and with whom, for that reason, I wanted to work. Adler and Sullivan were then building the Chicago Civic Auditorium, still the greatest room for opera in the world.

The tragedy befallen beloved architecture was still with me, Victor Hugo's prophecy often in mind. My sense of the tragedy had already bred in me hatred of the pilaster, the column for its own sake, the entablature, the cornice; in short all the architectural paraphernalia of the Renaissance. Only later did I come to know that Victor Hugo in the sweeping arc of his great thought had simply affirmed the truth: *Art can be no restatement.*


The great poet had foreseen that new uses of new materials by new inventions of new machine-methods would be devised and therefore great social changes become inevitable in the life of mankind. The poet saw that inherited styles and customs would undergo fundamental change in life and so in architecture: to make man ready to face reality anew in accord with "the great becoming." The inexorable Law of Change, by way of which the very flow of human life provides fresh inspiration, would compel new architecture, based upon Principle, to come alive.

The poet's message at heart, I wanted to go to work for the great moderns, Adler and Sullivan; and finally I went, warned by the prophecy and equipped, in fact armed, with the Froebel-kindergarten education I had received as a child from my mother. Early training which happened to be perfectly suited to the T-square and triangle technique now to become a characteristic, natural to the machine-age. Mother's intense interest in the Froebel system was awakened at the Philadelphia Centennial, 1876. In the Frederick Froebel Kindergarten exhibit there, mother found the "Gifts." And "gifts" they were. Along with the gifts was the system, as a basis for design and the elementary geometry behind all natural birth of Form.

Mother was a teacher who loved teaching; Father a preacher who loved and taught music. He taught me to see great symphony as a master's *edifice of sound*. Mother learned that Frederick Froebel taught that children should not be allowed to draw from casual appearances of Nature until they had first mastered the basic forms lying hidden behind appearances. Cosmic, geometric elements were what should first be made visible to the child-mind.

Taken East at the age of three to my father's pastorate near Boston, for several years I sat at the little kindergarten table-top ruled by lines about four inches apart each way making four-inch squares; and, among other things, played upon these "unit-lines" with the square (cube), the circle (sphere) and the triangle (tetrahedron or tripod) — these were smooth maple-wood blocks. Scarlet cardboard triangle (60°-30°) two inches on the short side, and one side white, were smooth triangular sections with which to come by pattern — design — by my own imagination. Eventually I was to construct designs in other mediums. But the smooth cardboard triangles and maple-wood blocks were most important. All are in my fingers to this day.

In outline the square was significant of integrity; the circle — infinity; the triangle — aspiration; all with which to "design" significant new forms. In the third dimension, the smooth maple blocks became the cube, the sphere and the tetrahedron; all mine to "play" with.

To reveal further subordinate, or encourage composite, forms these simple elemental blocks were suspended from a small gibbet by little wire inserts at the corners and whirled. On this simple unit-system ruled on the low table-top all these forms were combined by the child into imaginative pattern. Design was recreation!

Also German papers, glazed and matte, beautiful soft color qualities, were another one of the "gifts" — cut into sheets about twelve inches each way, these squares were slitted to be woven into gay colorful checkerings as fancy might dictate. Thus color sense awakened. There were also ingenious "constructions" to be made with straight, slender, pointed sticks like toothpicks or jack-straws, dried peas for the joinings, etc., etc. The virtue of all this lay in the awakening of the child-mind to rhythmic structure in Nature — giving the child a sense of innate cause-and-effect otherwise far beyond child-comprehension. I soon became susceptible to constructive pattern *evolving in everything I saw.* I learned to "see" this way and when I did, I did not care to draw casual incidentals of Nature. I wanted to *design.*

Later, when I was put to work as a teen-ager on my Uncle James' farm in the valley where I now live, this early habit of *seeing into and seeing from within* outward went on and on way beyond until at the age of nineteen when I presented myself as a novice to Mr. Sullivan I was already, and naturally, a potential designer with a T-square and triangle technique on a unit-system; the technique that could grow intimate with and master the rapacious characteristics of the Machine in consistent straight-line, flat-plane effects natural to machine technology, which then, as now, confronted all who were to build anything for modern life in America.


## THE CONFUSION

Among most of the architects I soon saw the great mother-art, architecture, completely confused when not demoralized. I saw their work as hackneyed or sentimentalized travesty of some kind; some old or limited eclecticism or the so-called "classic" of Beaux-Arts training encouraged by too many influential American Beaux-Arts graduates. The pilaster again!

But of the *Naissance* needed to replace moribund Renaissance I saw little or nothing outside the offices of Adler and Sullivan to take the place of the futility of restatement at least. Awakening was to come. Whoever then acknowledged the importance of art did not seem to know so well as we now know that art cannot be restatement. Against all this face-down servile perversion by education, encouraged by my early training at the kindergarten table and subsequent work on the farm in the valley, I came to feel that in the nature of Nature — if from within outward — I would come upon nothing not sacred. Nature had become my Bible.

Man the spiritual being, I now saw continually defeating himself — confusing his spiritual power with his mentality; his own beauty lost by his own stupidity or cupidity simply because he could not see from inside by his intellect alone: could not see the nature of his own intrinsic values: see his own genius, therefore. So during those days of early apprenticeship to Adler and Sullivan I found that when I talked about Nature I was not talking about the same thing those around me meant when they used the term. I could not fail to see (nearby was the Chicago Art Institute) each noble branch of the fine-arts family driven to filch what might be from the great wreck of architecture — the head of the regal family of art — and trying to make a go of it.

To survive, our American art was cheating itself of life. This consequent spread of the tragic Renaissance, I saw largely due to outworn but desperate reliance upon a dated formal professionalism: the Classic. This not alone in architecture but in all the arts; partly, perhaps mostly, due to the fearfully efficient tools, invented by Science, so abusing artists and abused by them. These new tools I saw wrecking the "classic" imitation of ancient formalism, called modern art but founded upon a philosophy completely false to modern life.

Human life itself was being cheated.

All was the same dire artificiality. Nature thus denied was more than ever revenging itself upon human life! The very soul of man was endangered. The Machine thus uncontrolled enlarged, and was living upon, these abuses. Already machine sytems had done deadly harm — and more harm, as things were then. Modern machine-masters were ruling man's fate in his manufactures as in his architecture and arts. His way of life was being sterilized by marvelous power-tools and even more powerful machine-systems, all replacing hand labor by multiplying — senselessly — his activity and infecting his spirit. Everywhere these inventions of science by ignorant misuse of a new technique were wiping out the artist. He was himself now becoming a slave. The new chattel. I saw in these new "masters" no great motive above the excess of necessity-for-profit; all likely themselves by way of their own assembly lines to become machines. The kind of slavery that now loomed was even more monstrous and more devastating to our culture now dedicated to senseless excess, so it seemed to me, than ever before. Slavery more deadly to human felicity than any yet devised. Unless in the competent artist's hand.

The pole-and-wire men in the name of social necessity had already forged a mortgage on the landscape of our beautiful American countryside while all our buildings, public and private, even churches, were senseless commitments to some kind of expediency instead of the new significances of freedom we so much needed. In the name of necessity, false fancy fronts hung with glaring signs as one trod along the miles of every urban sidewalk — instead of freedom, license — inextricable confusion. Trimmings and embellishments of trimmings pressed on the eye everywhere, made rampant by the casual taste of any ignoramus. These were all social liabilities forced upon American life by the misconception, or no conception at all, of the mother-art — architecture. Man, thus caricatured by himself — nature thus violated — invaded even the national forest-parks by a clumsy rusticity false to nature and so to architecture. The environment of civilized mankind was everywhere insulted by such willful stupidity.

But soon this saving virtue appeared to me in our disgraceful dilemma: Realization that any true cultural significance our American free society could know lay in the proper use of *the machine as a tool and used only as a tool*. But the creative-artist's use of mechanical systems, most beneficial miracles, was yet wholly missing.

22

# AWAKENING

Steel and glass themselves seemed to have come to use only to be misunderstood and misused, put to shame by such abuses as might be seen anywhere because they were everywhere.

In the plans and designs here presented in much detail may be seen the appropriate uses of the properties of steel in tension in relation to concrete (concrete the new-old plastic). With glass and the growing sheet-metal industries, these were, it seemed to me, only awaiting creative interpretation to become the body of our new democratic world: the same being true of new uses of the old materials — wood, brick and stone.

Often I sat down to write about this as well as continue to design new forms for these new methods and materials. Occasionally, when invited, I went out to speak on the subject of the proper use of all these — always to say "we must know better the here and now of *our own* life in its Time and Place. In all we must learn to see ourselves as we are, as *modern* man — and this be our true culture." As architects young and old we owed this to ourselves, and certainly to our people. In this country of ours we were free now to abandon outdated idiosyncrasy in the name of taste, or arbitrary academic formalisms without thought or feeling — and learn to show, by our own work, our love and consequent understanding of the principles of Nature. Life *indigenous* was now to be embodied in new forms and more significant uses; new forms of materials by the inevitable new machine-methods yet missing or misunderstood. A natural heretic, I declared these materials and methods to be in themselves a new potential needed in the culture of modern life. Because of the machine itself, architecture was now bound by its own nature to be prophetic. The architect's interpretations would show the way to the right use of these great new organic resources. Our new facilities were already capable of inspiring and enriching human life if provided with true forms, instead of perpetually inciting American life to folly and betrayal of its own nature by ignorant or silly eclecticism or any of the 57 fashionable Varieties of the day. Despite artificial limitations, a new beauty would be ours. Thus awakening to action, we architects had to become effective soon — or our civilization would destroy its chances for its own culture. Instead of by the handle, man had taken this dangerous new tool by the blade!

## REALIZATION

In this sense I saw the architect as savior of the culture of modern American society; his services the mainspring of any future cultural life in America — savior now as for all civilizations heretofore. Architecture being inevitably the basis of an indigenous culture, American architects must become emancipators of senselessly conforming human beings imposed upon by mediocrity and imposing mediocrity upon others in this sanitary but soulless machine-age. Architecture, I believed, was bound to become more humanely significant because of these vast new facilities. Therefore not only special but social knowledge of the nature of architecture as presenting man himself, must be greatly expanded. Architecture was to be liberated from all formalistic stylizing by any elite, especially from that perpetuated by scholastic architects or by the criteria of insolent criticism. Architecture of the machine-age should become not only fundamental to our culture but natural to the happiness of our lives in it as well. All this was rank heresy at the time. We have made some progress since because it does not seem so heretical now.

Young heretic, then, I freely spoke but steadily planned all the time: hope of realization firmly at heart — pretty well in mind now, as poetry. I loved architecture as romantic and prophetic of a true way of life; life again coming beautifully alive today as before in the greatest ancient civilizations. We were free men now? The architect among us then should qualify as so inspired; be free leader of free human beings in our new free country. All buildings built should serve the liberation of mankind, liberating the lives of *individuals*. What amazing beauty would be ours if man's spirit, thus organic, should learn to characterize this new free life of ours in America as natural!

## RETROGRESSION

But soon I saw the new resources not only shamefully wasted by machinesters but most shamefully wasted by our influential architects them-

Drawing shown to lieber Meister
when applying for a job —

1888. "DRAWING SHOWN TO LIEBER MEISTER WHEN APPLYING FOR A JOB."

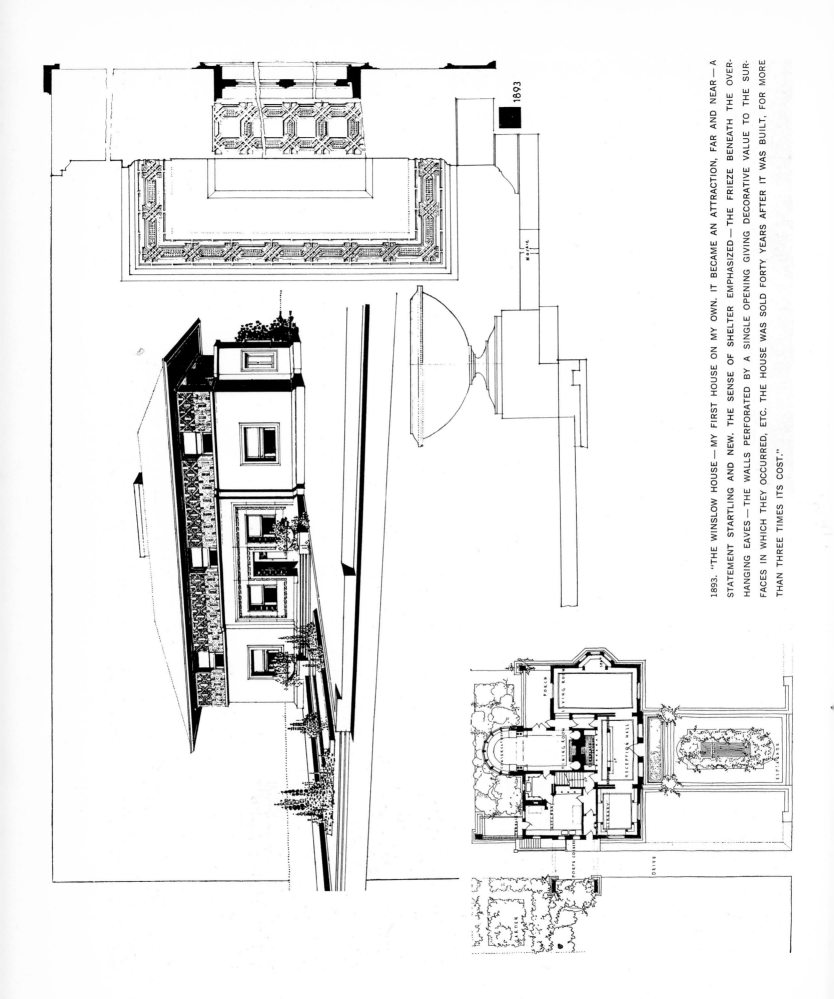

1893. "THE WINSLOW HOUSE — MY FIRST HOUSE ON MY OWN. IT BECAME AN ATTRACTION, FAR AND NEAR — A STATEMENT STARTLING AND NEW. THE SENSE OF SHELTER EMPHASIZED — THE FRIEZE BENEATH THE OVER-HANGING EAVES — THE WALLS PERFORATED BY A SINGLE OPENING GIVING DECORATIVE VALUE TO THE SUR-FACES IN WHICH THEY OCCURRED, ETC. THE HOUSE WAS SOLD FORTY YEARS AFTER IT WAS BUILT, FOR MORE THAN THREE TIMES ITS COST."

1895.  FRANK LLOYD WRIGHT STUDIO, OAK PARK, ILL.

OUTER OFFICE

DRAUGHTING ROOM

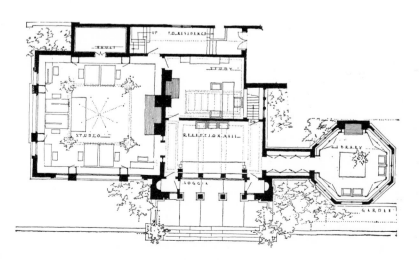

1897. "THIS LUXFER PRISM FACADE IN GLASS AND CONCRETE WAS DESIGNED FOR A CHICAGO OFFICE BUILD-
ING. IT HAS SINCE APPEARED IN MANY GUISES IN MANY COUNTRIES. A TYPE OF FACADE NOW FASHIONABLE."

1896. "ROMEO AND JULIET" — WINDMILL FOR MISSES LLOYD JONES, HILLSIDE, SPRING GREEN, WISCONSIN. SECTION BELOW

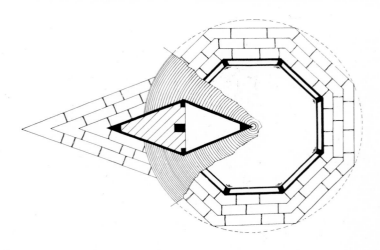

1897. PROJECT, DESIGN FOR MOTION PICTURE THEATRE

selves; those with the best educations were most deadly. Our resources were being used to ruin the significance of any true architecture of the life of our own day by ancient ideas imposed upon modern building or ancient building ruined by so-called "modern" ideas. Thus played upon, some better architects, then called modern, were themselves desperately trying to reorganize American building and themselves as well. The A.I.A., then composed of architects who came down the hard way, was inclined to be sincere, but the plan-factory was already appearing as public enemy number one.

I had just opened my own office in the Schiller Building, 1893, when came disaster — Chicago's first World's Fair. The fair soon appeared to me more than ever tragic travesty: florid countenance of theoretical Beaux-Arts formalisms; perversion of what modern building we then had achieved by negation; already a blight upon our progress. A senseless reversion. Nevertheless at that time — now more than sixty years ago — I was myself certain that awakening in our own architecture was just around the turn of the corner of the next year. That year I wrote *The Art and Craft of the Machine*, delivering the essay at Hull House by Jane Addams' invitation. Next day a Chicago Tribune editorial announced that an American artist had said the first word for the appropriate use of the machine as an artist's tool. I suspect that Jane Addams wrote the editorial herself.

By this time the American people had become sentimentally enamored of the old-lace, nervous artificiality of the "classic" grandomania endorsed by the A.I.A. at the fair. It was everywhere in evidence: excess — as usual — mistaken for exuberance. Owing to this first World's Fair, recognition of organic American architecture would have to wait at least another half-century.


## "THE CHICAGO SCHOOL"

No school exists without something to teach; and until the phrase "Chicago School" appeared so many years later, I was not aware that anything like a "school" had existed. At the time, there was a small group composed of my own adherents and of contemporary dissenters by nature. The work of Adler and Sullivan was in constant contrast to the work of Richardson and Root; later, Shepley, Rutan and Coolidge (heirs of Richardson), but few of the architects, young or old, then admitted the Adler and Sullivan influence.

Because I was, so far as they were concerned, Sullivan's "alter ego," a small clique soon formed about me, myself naturally enough the leader. Friendships were formed in those early days, especially after the gold letters ARCHITECT were put upon the plate glass door of my office in The Schiller Building. The "followers" were not many: first among them Cecil Corwin and Robert C. Spencer, Jr. (Bob) — first converts to the new architecture. Bob was regarded by his "classic" comrades as apostate because his employers — Shepley, Rutan and Coolidge — had gone "classic" soon after the romantic Richardson's death. Bob and I were often seen together; later he took the office next mine in the Schiller. Chicago conformists working in other offices, seeing us arm in arm down the street, would say in derision, "There goes God-almighty with his Jesus Christ." Bob didn't mind. He stuck. Some others began to "come around": George Dean, Hugh Garden, Myron Hunt, Dwight Perkins, Dick Schmidt and Howard Shaw; all were friendly but not willing to cut their umbilical cord to the Colonial or the French chateau, the English manor house or the grando-mania of Beaux-Arts days.

Before long a little luncheon club formed, comprised of myself, Bob Spencer, Gamble Rogers, Handy and Cady, Dick Schmidt, Hugh Garden, Dean, Perkins and Shaw, several others; eighteen in all. We called the group the "Eighteen."

The "Eighteen" often wanted to know how I convinced my clients that the new architecture was the right thing. "Do you hypnotize them?" was a common question. The idea of an American architecture fascinated them to a certain degree according to the nature of their understanding. Almost all admired what I was doing though they were not yet willing to say it was the right thing.

Gamble Rogers never left the Gothic; Howard Shaw never dared leave colonial English. But most of the others fell in with the idea of some sort of modern architecture. I became original advisory exemplar to the group.

The little luncheon round-table broke up after a year or two. I with those nearest me rented a vacant loft in Steinway Hall: a building Dwight Perkins had built. But Spencer, Perkins, Hunt and Birch Long (clever boy renderer) moved in with me. Together we subdivided the big attic into studio-like draughting rooms. We felt the big attic especially appropriate for our purpose. We each had a share in a receptionist and stenographer in common as "office force" on the floor below, trying to please us all. The entrance door panel was a single sheet of clear plate glass, the second one in existence, like the entrance door to the Schiller offices, with all our names thereon in the same kind of gold letters.

By this time an increasing number of young draughtsmen, like Max Dunning et al, began to come around. I got Lieber Meister to address the Chicago Architectural Sketch-Club, which he did with great effect. Dankmar Adler was dean of the A.I.A. at the time, and he also wrote valuable papers on the subject of skyscraper construction, and the effect of steel on modern life. Meantime, buildings were going up under "the Adler and Sullivan influence." A little of the new was worked in by others here and there. But all in all, from my impatient standpoint, weak if not impotent or cowardly. On occasion, I did say so, but patiently worked on their plans when I could be helpful. My most enthusiastic advocate, young Myron Hunt, was first among them to set up in Evanston, Illinois, as a "modern," with the building of the "White" house. That was a characteristic instance. I believed myself helpful to them all.

I remember an ebullient Italian, Boari by name, who won the competition to build the National Grand Opera House in Mexico City. He came into our attic space, temporarily, to make plans for that edifice. He was far from all of us but observing, curious and humorous. He would look at something I was doing and say with a good natured grunt, "Huh, temperance-architecture!" turn on his heel with another grunt and go back to his Italian Renaissance "gorge" as I called it in retaliation. What he was then doing is now there in Mexico City but badly affected by the universal settlements going on because of the lowering of the water-level beneath the city.

Other work went on in our studio-loft for several more years. But when I had left Adler and Sullivan to settle down in Oak Park, Bob had moved out to River Forest, the next suburb to the west. I — the amateur still with Adler and Sullivan — was able to build a little house on Chicago Avenue; and, on my own, built a studio adjoining my home, where the work I had then to do enabled me to take in several draughtsmen and a faithful secretary, Isabel Roberts, for whom I later built a dwelling in River Forest, now owned by and revised for the Scotts.

But by that time at Oak Park I had lost touch with most of the original group. Into the now flourishing Oak Park studio had come Walter Griffin, Marion Mahoney (later married to Walter), William Drummond, George Willis, Andrew Willatzen, Frank Byrne, Albert McArthur. Others came and went as time went along.

By that time, 1894-5, architecture so-called "modern" had made sporadic appearances here and there around Chicago; reminiscent of Lieber Meister's ornament or something I had myself done or was doing as a dwelling.

George Elmslie — I had brought George from Silsbee's as my understudy (lasting the seven years I remained with Adler and Sullivan and staying on for many more years) — would sometimes come out to lend us a hand in the Oak Park studio, putting in overtime when pressure of work would keep us all up all night, and the dawn would find the boys asleep on their draughting boards.

But, now independent, I didn't use the fascinating ornament, had struck out a new line in a field of my own — the American dwelling: the nature of materials and steel in tension. Of what was going on abroad at this time I had no knowledge nor any interest in. Nor was there any Japanese architectural influence, as may be seen in these illustrations.


## DISASTER

Schools of thought, to and fro, soon arose in America — one of them misled by the dictum "Art is art precisely in that it is not nature"; misunderstanding the word "nature." This was really art for art's sake? "Form follows function" came along now also to become the new slogan (also misunderstood). But art was not as yet transferred to the region of the mere nervous system; the nervous system had not yet been mistaken for the soul. But little men were using little brains and little-finger sensibility to confect semblances that "tasted" to them like inspiration, confections mistaken for architecture. All but several architects seemed to be trying to annul the idea of architecture as noble organic expression of nature; the Form-Follows-Function group seeing it as a physical raw-materialism instead of the spiritual thing it really is: the idea of life itself — bodily and spiritually — intrinsic *organism*. Form and function as one.

Well — Daniel H. Burnham was right. The Chicago World's Fair became the occasion of modern architecture's grand relapse. The nature of man was there reduced to the level of a clever trained animal: Architecture contrived as a hackneyed ruse to cheat modern life of its divine due instead of serving to glorify it. Beaux-Arts intellectualism was the aesthetic that could only eventuate as some kind of menial to the monumental. Therefore "classic" misuse of the "Classic" slandered the noble idea of art as organic, and I was compelled to see that it would go on so long as man had no true sense of his own dignity as a free man. Only if his intellect, which had been stimulated but pauperized by education, again became subject to the inner laws of his own being, could he be a valid force in Architecture, Art or in Religion: only so could he ever rise creative above our inventive sciences in the grasp of the Expedient. Otherwise his life in America would remain helplessly afloat upon a sea of corrupted taste; no realization would be possible.

## CONTRIBUTION

When man's pride in his own intellect was set up as an anti-nature-formalism in art, he became responsible for the dictum: "where every prospect pleases and only man is vile."

Different were the Orientals and different were Jesus, Shakespeare, Milton, Blake, Wordsworth, Coleridge, Keats, Shelley, Beethoven, Bach, Brunelleschi, Goethe, Rembrandt, Dante, Cervantes, Giotto, Mantegna, Leonardo, Bramante, Angelo. Different were the prophets of the human soul. All masters of the Nature of Man and the hosts they have inspired. No longer trying to lift himself by his boot-straps or busy cutting out the head of his drum to see whence comes the sound, man by nature still creative may grow.

## MAN AND THE MACHINE

As Victor Hugo wrote also in *Notre Dame,* Gutenberg's invention of shifting-type *was* the beginning of the great triumph of the machine over all the fine-arts and crafts of architecture. By way of the machine came the soulless monstrosities now so far out of human scale as to be out of hand. Death came to handicraft and to any corresponding culture in the world, blindly inherited by us. As for America, cultural confusion had already come upon us in our new "house," almost before we were born. Buildings, business, education — all were becoming great enterprises stimulated by infatuations with science and sentimentality concerning the past. The inventive engineering of mechanization lacked the insight — creative poetic imagination, let's say — to recognize the power of interpretation by architecture of these vast new facilities. As they came fresh from science, they but stimulated the cupidity of commerce. As for the architects, they were either silent or huddled in the lap of overpowering change. Our capitalism was a kind of piracy, our profit-system tended to encourage low forms of avaricious expansion. American culture, such as it was, wore a false face, a hideous masquerade. Success was misunderstood as essential to progress. Really success was worse than failure. Wanton denials of humanity were made by machine-power, abetted by the impotence of artists and architects, themselves blind to the fresh opportunities, really their duties. Such failures as they were making of life, then as now, were a standardized slander upon the liberated individual rather than any true reflection of his innate power. Thus doomed to spiritual sterility, art and architecture were facing extinction in all the hell there was.

Well, nevertheless — rather more — I kept on planning, preaching, presenting the real social need for the creative artist-architect — the competent, conscientious interpreter of his kind and time! But where were such architects? Was the A.I.A. alive to the new ideals? The story by now might have been different if the A.I.A. had not been more interested in architects than in architecture. In such circumstances how could the architect's vision become effective action? Could action come to grips with selfish forces to humanize their excesses by rejecting their power, to evolve the new forms modern man needed to sustain the freedom he had declared, 1776? This was up to the greater architect we had neither inherited nor cultivated. Because of this default I kept trying to gather together the dangling, loose ends, so twisted by this confusion; gather them little by little into organic synthesis of means to ends, thus showing with all my might the idea and purpose of organic character and proportions in building, if made appropriate to life under American Democracy.

*New* architecture was fundamental necessity. But it seemed impossible for architecture to rise without deeper knowledge of the poetic principle involved. The slide-rule of the engineer could not diminish, but only cherish and confirm, all this damnation — and did so.

The needed interpretation had arrived in my own mind as organic and, being true to nature would naturally, so I thought, be visible to my fellow architects. In spite of myself, because becoming more and more articulate, I became a kind of troublesome reminder — a reproach to my fellows. Naturally enough I would not join the profession to help make a harbor of refuge for the incompetent? So, deemed arrogant even by those who might have been expected to go a little deeper and go to work themselves, I had to go it pretty much alone — Lieber Meister gone.

## THE FIELD

Among the architects practising in America when I entered Adler and Sullivan's offices, Richardson had the high honor of the field; Beaux-Arts graduate, Bostonian well-connected with the better elements of society, the Adamses, etc. But Richardson had robust appetite for romance. His Romanesque soon overthrew prevailing preferences for Renaissance. Eventually he became the most productive and successful of those men, the great eclectics of their time. Many of them fell in love with his love of the Romanesque. Yes, his Romanesque soon amounted to something wherever his fellow architects were concerned with a style.

Louis Sullivan himself kept an eye upon Richardson's superb use of stone in the arch. H. H. Richardson's use of the arch in early days, "but not his ornament," had a visible effect upon Lieber Meister. Richardson disciples were legion; his success was tremendous. Henry Hobson Richardson, though an artist and giving signs of emerging as modern, was just what America deserved most but should have had least — a powerful romantic eclectic. Gone now.

McKim, Mead and White, Richardson's elite running competition, were also Beaux-Arts men. Their eclecticism was of another more elegant order, faithful to the more choice effects of early Italian (moyen-age or better-day) Renaissance. In their affected cultivated stride they took the ancient buildings verbatim. Whenever they found the buildings they admired, they copied them, enlarging the details by lantern slide. Used them straight. Their following was, of course, automatically more socially elite than Richardson's but extensive. Gone now.

Richard M. Hunt, darling of New York's four hundred, head of their procession on Fifth and other American avenues, was a good technician with a finished preference for the French-Gothic ensemble. He was fashionable, too, his eclecticisms immensely popular and profitable to him. But not to America. Gone now.

There was another much less idolized group, to which Adler and Sullivan, Major Jenney, John Root, Cass Gilbert, Van Brunt and Howe and several others, belonged. Of them the only men indicating genius above engineering ability and the capabilities of front-men were Louis Sullivan and John Root. Of Root it might be said that Sullivan was slightly envious because the two firms, Adler and Sullivan and Burnham and Root, were in direct competition, the latter firm having the best of it. Then Root's office building, the Monadnock of Chicago, might be put against Louis Sullivan's Wainwright of St. Louis. Although the Monadnock arose later, it was vital too, but an unsuitable forcing of the material: brick. See the unbricklike molded corners.

The strain of genius in Root was far less than the miracle of genius in Sullivan. Unfortunately Root barely survived the Chicago World's Fair, in the planning of which he had a major hand, supported as he was by the great master-manager, his partner Daniel H. Burnham, head architect of the Fair. He, "Uncle Dan" ("make no little plans") would have been equally great in the hat, cap or shoe business.

Of young aspirants at the time there were many, mostly head-draughtsmen like myself. There were also independents like S. S. Beman, J. L. Silsbee and many other talented men in the offices of the Middle West and of the East, such men as the Beaux-Arts Carrère and Hastings, etc., etc.

1900. PROJECT, A HOME IN A PRAIRIE TOWN, FOR LADIES' HOME JOURNAL.
BELOW: GROUND FLOOR PLAN, LEFT — SECOND FLOOR PLAN AT RIGHT

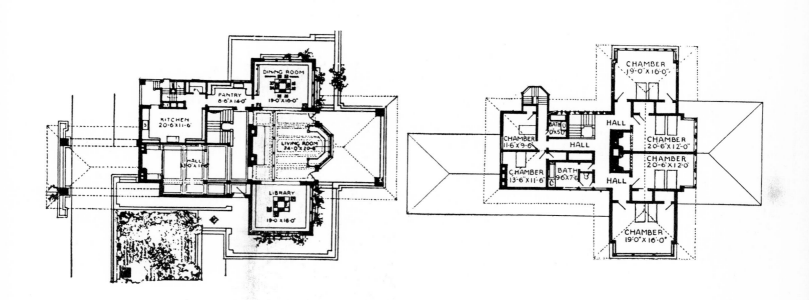

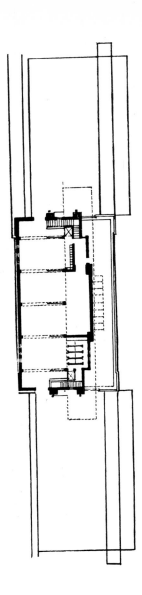

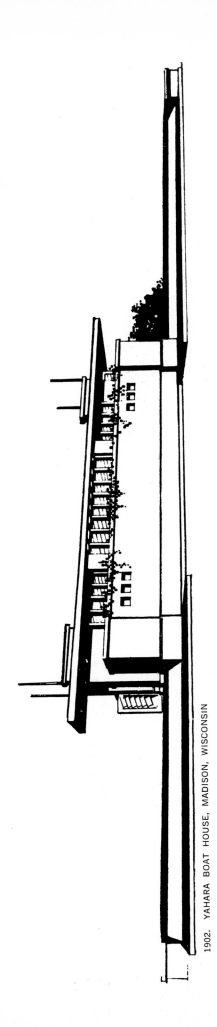

1902. YAHARA BOAT HOUSE, MADISON, WISCONSIN

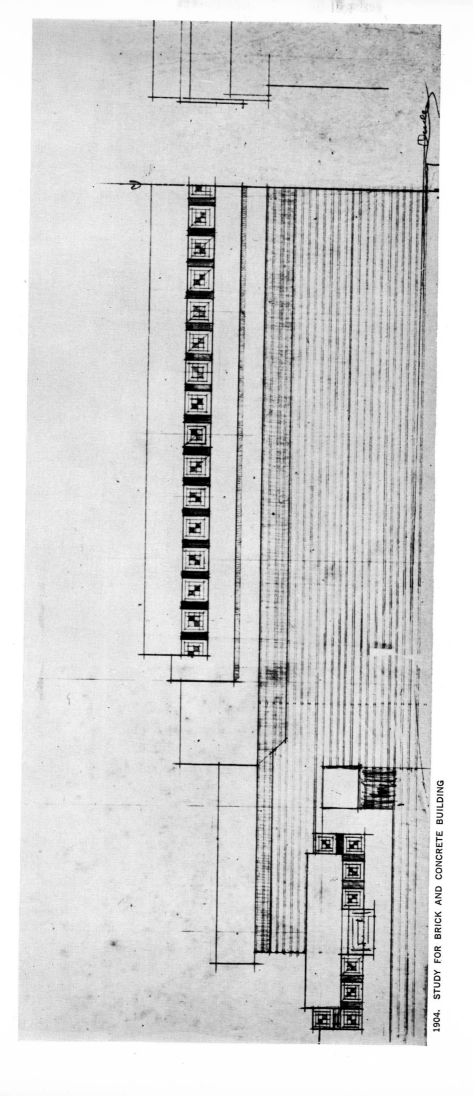

1904. STUDY FOR BRICK AND CONCRETE BUILDING

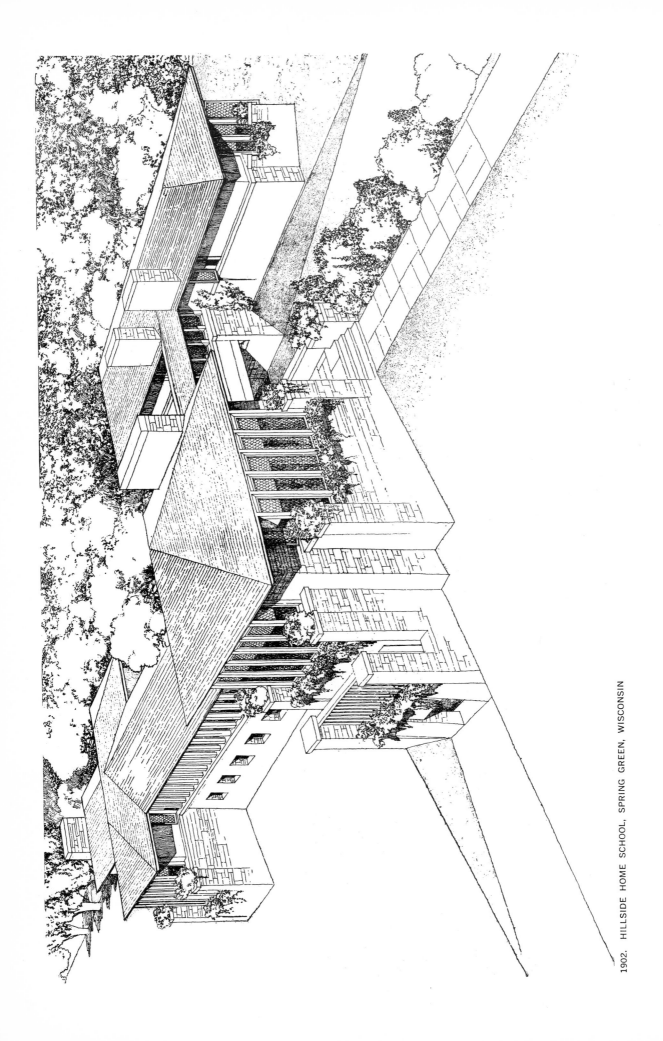

1902. HILLSIDE HOME SCHOOL, SPRING GREEN, WISCONSIN

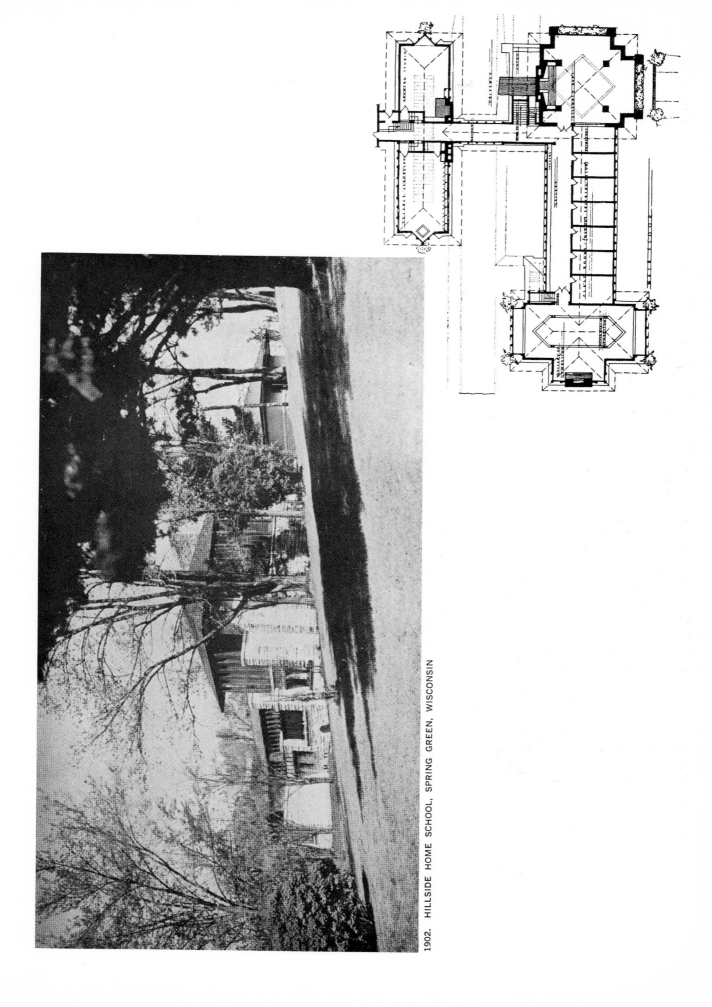

1902. HILLSIDE HOME SCHOOL, SPRING GREEN, WISCONSIN

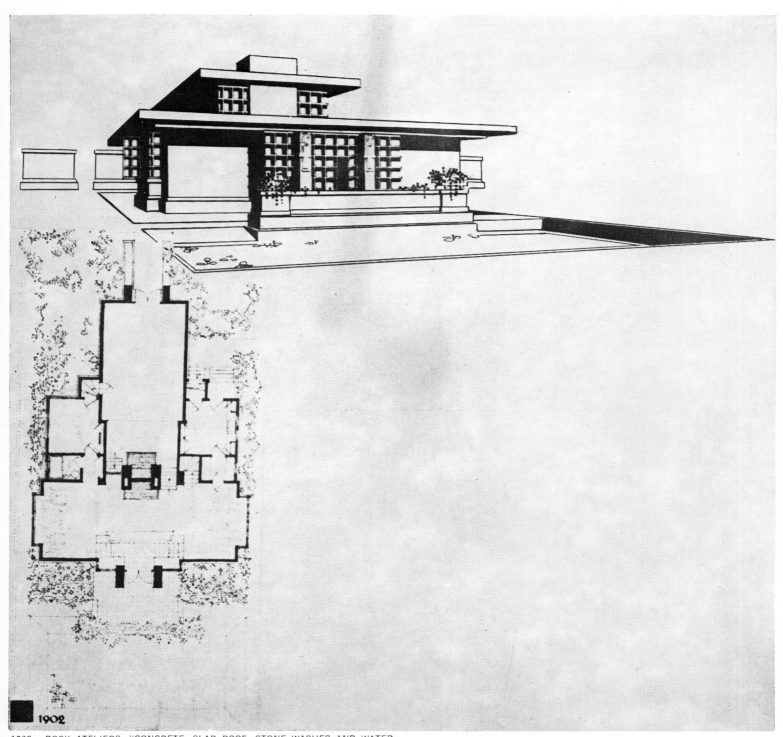

1902. BOCK ATELIERS. "CONCRETE. SLAB ROOF. STONE WASHES AND WATER
TABLE. WINDOWS WRAPPING CORNERS TO EXPRESS INTERIOR SPACE."

1902.  HEURTLEY HOUSE, OAK PARK, ILLINOIS
GROUND FLOOR PLAN BELOW, LEFT — SECOND FLOOR PLAN AT RIGHT

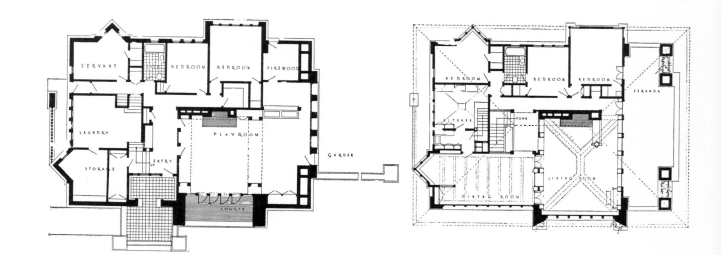

1904. THE LARKIN BUILDING, BUFFALO, NEW YORK. "A FIREPROOF, AIR-CONDITIONED BUILDING FUR-
NISHED THROUGHOUT WITH STEEL. FIRST IN MANY WAYS — ALL-GLASS DOORS, DOUBLE GLASS WINDOWS,
COMPLETE AIR-CONDITIONING, ESPECIALLY DESIGNED STEEL FILING SYSTEMS, STEEL DESK FURNITURE
AND SEATS, TELEPHONES AND LIGHTING SYSTEM ESPECIALLY DESIGNED IN STEEL, ETC. BUILDING DE-
MOLISHED IN 1950."

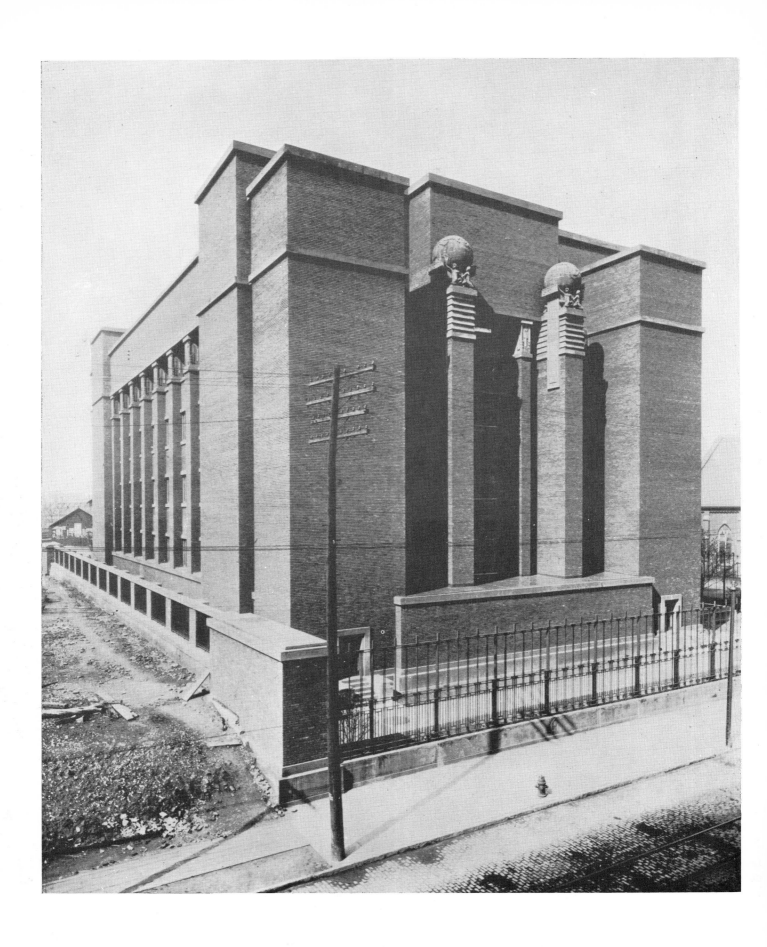

1904. THE LARKIN BUILDING, BUFFALO, NEW YORK — SIDE VIEW AND OFFICE INTERIOR

1904. CHENEY HOUSE, OAK PARK, ILLINOIS. "DESIGNED WHEN I WAS STILL WITH ADLER AND SULLIVAN IN 1893 — BUILT SEVERAL YEARS LATER." FIRST SKETCH (ABOVE), PLAN AND PERSPECTIVE

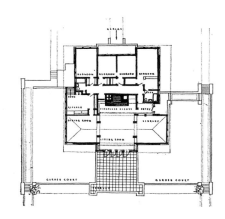

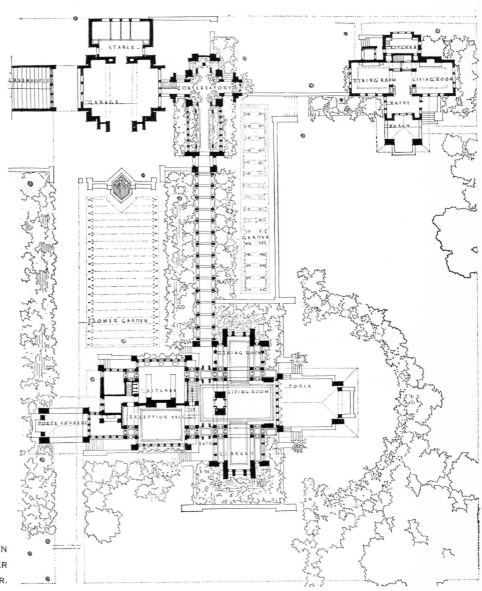

1904. MARTIN HOUSE, BUFFALO, NEW YORK. PLAN ALSO INCLUDES THE BARTON HOUSE (UPPER RIGHT) BUILT FOR MR. MARTIN'S DAUGHTER.

1905.  HARDY HOUSE, RACINE, WISCONSIN

STREET FRONT

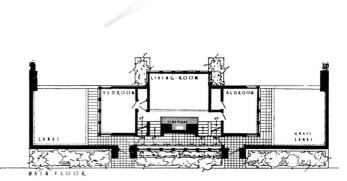

MAIN FLOOR PLAN

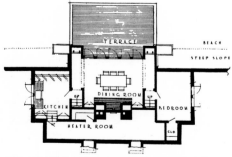

TOP (MEZZANINE) FLOOR PLAN ABOVE, LOWER
FLOOR PLAN BELOW. AT RIGHT: PERSPECTIVE
FROM LAKE

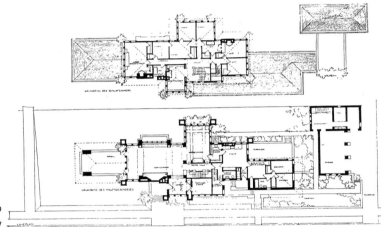

1905. HEATH HOUSE, BUFFALO, NEW YORK. SECOND
FLOOR PLAN AT TOP, MAIN FLOOR PLAN BELOW

The Chicago World's Fair was a procession of this talent that brought these leaders of their profession out into the open. Their merits and defects might be there seen and appraised. Due largely to "Uncle Dan" Burnham's ("Frank, the Fair shows our people the beauty of the Classic — they will never go back")* ability to promote ideas of Charles McKim et al, the Fair reopened wide the case for European Renaissance, and America had a memorable field day à la Paris Beaux-Arts. The "Classic" easily won and the more pertinacious and influential among the more successful architects of the A.I.A. were for the time being almost totally in command. "The eye of the vox-populi" (as a popular Fourth of July orator once put it) opened wide in dreamy-eyed wonder at the Chicago World's Fair. The ambitious ignoramus in the architectural profession throughout America was captivated. The old, old story! By this overwhelming rise of grandomania I was confirmed in my fear that a native architecture would be set back at least fifty years.

But Louis Sullivan's Transportation Building was the only picture building at the Fair presented by the Paris Beaux-Arts itself with its distinguished gold medal; which must have astonished the Beaux-Arts society of America. A society of which the original French Beaux-Arts seemed not to think highly, as I learned long years later, 1940.

Such in broad outline was the rough contour of the A.I.A. during my apprenticeship with Adler and Sullivan. There in the Adler and Sullivan offices high in the Chicago Auditorium Tower I worked for nearly seven years — George Elmslie alongside — occasionally looking out through the romantic Richardsonian Romanesque arches over Lake Michigan or often, after dark, watching the glow of giant Bessemer Steel converters reddening the night sky down towards South Chicago. I looked from those high-up arches down upon the great, growing city of Chicago as the Illinois Central trains puffed along the lake front.

---

* Daniel H. Burnham to Frank Lloyd Wright.

# CIVILIZATION AS ABSTRACTION

This abstraction we are calling Civilization — how was it made and how is it misused or being lost now? By "abstraction" I mean taking the essence of a thing — anything — *the pattern of it*, as the substance of reality. Incidental effects aside, the *heart* of the matter would lie in the abstraction if well made, and nature truly interpreted — expressed in pattern by the true artist: Linear and spatial significance of the reality *within* — this is what is patterned forth. If thus intrinsic, this is the artist's contribution to his society: truly the *creative* artist's affair. Our customs, costumes, habits, habitations and manners, all are, or should be, such abstractions; and made, as such, true to the great abstraction we call civilization. That, genuine, would be our culture. If the abstraction is truly made well above the animal nature in man — his gregarious nature — it will keep the ancient rituals of his higher nature as long as possible. Human abstractions if true usually become rituals. Once made, although the ritual may become "obsolete," the original abstraction will be cherished by man because the rituals recorded what his kind once considered beautiful to see, to feel, to hear or to know. Sometimes all together.

This retention of the abstract as beautiful goes to the extent that few now living can distinguish in those abstractions (civilizations now dead) what differs essentially from those still alive. "Taste" still meanders about among them all — confused as it is in this vast forest of the ancient abstract. "Taste," waif or prostitute, lost in the interminable stretches of the abstract. We therefore need the prophet always to make new abstractions for life more in accord with the eternal Law of Change. This is largely the service the creative architect renders to his society, now no less than ever. The service he alone may render with conscience, justice and lustre.

What means more to the life of the individual in our own place in Time than this study of the nature of human nature, the search to discover pertinent traces of hidden impulses of life, to form continually new abstractions uplifting the life he lives? From such intensive introversion issues inestimable treasure for extroversion in interpreting his civilization. This, alone, justifies the trust that society must repose in the architect if creative. The true architect is a poet who will someday discover in himself the presence of the tomorrow in our today.

## POET—"Unacknowledged legislator of the world"

Then, as now, I knew that he alone could have the inspiring insight needed to give human society true answers — answers always related to philosophy continually new. Yes, I knew, even then, that the revelations American society needed to go with our new declaration of faith in man could not possibly come from science. Except for Louis Sullivan among the many poets I knew and have named, there were then none among all the architects of this world. The poet had been too long absent from architecture. So long indeed, architecture was no longer considered as a great creative art. But where might the soul of any humane culture we might ever know be found unless in architecture?

Thoreau, Emerson, were ours. Yes. And then, too, Walt Whitman came to view to give needed religious inspiration in the great change: our new Place for the new Man in our Time. Walt Whitman, seer of our Democracy! He uttered primitive truths lying at the base of our new life, the inspirations we needed to go on spiritually with the brave "sovereignty of the individual." Might not the *spirit* of creative art, desperately needed by man, lie in the proper use of the radical new technologies of our times, and so arise? Not from, nor by, any established authority whatsoever, nor any religious sectarianisms. This kind of inspiration was nothing to expect from the committee-mind or from any officialdom. I well knew it was not there. Sixty years ago I knew that until the needed inspiration could be found forthcoming in architecture — enlightened instead of conditioned in this realm we have been calling Education — we would probably look in vain for coherent interpretation of our time and our place in time.

Consider that the United States of America appeared 160 years ago with this unique, inspiring message that started a world revolution in government. Freedom for the human being to be his better self! Reflect that man thus became the unit of a civilization itself *individual*. See how inspired and brave were our founders. What courage then to declare *officially a nation* of people free! Consider too: Were American freemen conscious of being newborn to the mundane society of this world, how inevitable to America, then, was great art and so as its basis a genuine architecture. *Organic* to go with the nature of that Declaration! Organic architecture based upon this new faith, not only faith in mankind's manhood but faith in the man as himself *creative;* man always greater than any system he might ever devise! Therein fresh opportunity came to us. Modern man enabled to conceive and achieve a new harmony with life. New hope now for a man to improve himself — *as himself*: to serve with good conscience the new idea of State according to his ability. Men were now bound to *grow*; to become useful leaders in their own time, in their own country, because they were now free to use and be used by their fellows each to each preserving the integrity and beauty of life for each and so for all. This was what our new democracy, as a form of government, meant? Heresy when it was declared. A quandary even now?

## CONFORMITY

Unfortunately conformity reaches far and wide into American life: to distort our democracy? This drift toward quantity instead of quality is largely distortion. Conformity is always too convenient? Quality means *individuality,* is therefore difficult. But unless we go deeper now, quantity at expense to quality will be our national tragedy — the rise of mediocrity into high places.

Servility increases — already a seemingly unguarded danger to democracy not only in art and architecture and religion but in all phases of life. Between the radical and the conformist lies all the difference between a lithe tendon and a length of gas-pipe.

Because of this all the more, it was for illustrious *sovereignty of the individual* that I wanted to build. Too little of the beautiful had ever been built for man's personal life on earth and nothing whatever by government with the depth of understanding essential to this new ideal of manhood. So, 1921, I wrote (badly) *The Disappearing City,* followed this later by *When Democracy Builds,* prophesying and promoting the inevitable American City of tomorrow — ours if democracy is to survive. At least I did succeed in outlining what I thought would be the center-line in building democratic man into his environment according to his new ideals of government, by means of his amazing new scientific leverage: the machine. Planning the new city now became organic: organic building design and construction. This new city belonging to America also to accord with our political Declaration. Accordingly, Taliesin (1932) modeled Broadacre City. I saw it coming as an irresistible current to vindicate new uses of science and bring closer to reality the new vision of man's social integrity as an individual. I had learned to see the right use of machine-craft as a living element in the organism of our society — and therefore bound to come right side up in the American City. I saw this new city denying all enforced formalisms in any style whatsoever. I saw our big cities as the overgrown villages they are — over-invested, under-engineered, unclassified, the outmembered, over-numbered, over-gadgeted cliché of antiquity. European civilizations of the Middle Ages had left us our city and we had done nothing with it but cram it with gadgetry. We, the last word in progress, were still back there with Sodom and Gomorrah. See the chapter in Genesis where Cain, the murderer of his brother, went forth with his sons to found the city. The City still murdering his brother.

## NEW THOUGHT

Other than the declaration of the master-poet of our world: "The Kingdom of God is within *you*," it seemed to me that organic architecture was the only visible evidence of this in modern art. Old definitions were sadly lacking perspective anywhere; new definitions were now imperative all down the line: definitions long past due in religion as well as art. This new-old philosophy, too — and therefore — had to appear if we were ever to experience inspiring creation and — soon enough — find a basis for the free culture we might honestly call our own. We the American people would learn to develop a true humane joy in the environment of our daily life, and achieve beauty of life — the home as a work of art part of this vision. This, despite all confusions, I saw wrought by and for the self-hood of the individual. But confusions of the public "taste" were only increased by self-made, self-willed, self-styled critics, also an affliction by "taste." I then believed critics were by nature no less confused than confusing.

Were I as an architect to work thus for the Beautiful — I loved the idea of "romantic" — in the everyday American city and the country by myself, my first thought must be a valid social science, a conscious point of view in society: philosophic thought basic to democracy, organic planning no less basic to a new architecture fit for the machine-age. What necessarily then, would such organic planning be? Naturally true to our Declaration: thought free. Not only the artist's motive free but also the *political* basis of the democracy we love as an ideal made valid and try to believe we still desire, free.

## ROMANCE—THE FREE PHILOSOPHY

Comes to our American view, then, the highest form of aristocracy yet known — the highest because *innate*: Aristocracy natural as the quality of the man himself, no longer *on* him but *of* him: aristocracy his, not by way of privilege nor inheritance, but truly his: a quality developed from within himself. Unique.

The ancient American architectures of the Inca, the Mayan and the Toltec are lying centuries deep buried in the earth where ages ago instead of the free soul of man, the cosmic-order of sun, moon and stars inspired primitive man to level mountains and erect great temples to his material power.

Again in America we erect temples but this time not so much to the mystery of great terrestrial or cosmic forces as to the interior or spirit-power of manhood as released by American democracy and its sciences. How much greater is this new expression of the soul of man! A new light may shine from every edifice built by the human mind.

## JEFFERSON'S ARISTOI

Thomas Jefferson prophesied the democratic Aristoi. We his people must now not only meet the radical changes in our political and social systems but face no less these changes in the basis of our culture. If integrity of spirit inheres in man, its natural countenance will be found in his architecture: the countenance of principle. Because architecture presents man as he is, he will live anew in the free spirit of organic architecture of our own time.

New, but still natural, interpretations of man in a living architecture thus become our privilege. A new abstraction, as civilization, arises to express the new life-of-man as free. He is yet a changeling of tide and time. This I believed long ago even as I became an architect, trained at the kindergarten table. So nearly everything I saw standing outside myself — man-made — had to be *new*. How could buildings any longer be of past or future "schools" so-called? There could now never be schools! Schools could only be remade and so be makeshifts: old cultures that were originally in themselves eclecticisms.

But now for us must come an America neither modern cliché nor ancient classic. Nor any habitual repetitions, restatements, restorations, under which the spirit of man has so long languished to disintegrate. For 500 years at least, these pressures of temporal authority have prevailed. The old manipulations of mankind by authority, politics, fashions, academic pressures, prevailed but were not really authentic.

Fresh cultural life, now to issue from the "reality within," begins a new world!


## INTEGRITY

Meantime many contumacious substitutes have arisen and more will arise. A natural or organic architecture, as modern, has already been misused. Much perversity has been extolled, admired as expedient. Worthless architectural facades in novel materials are now commercial posters — hailed by the "avant garde" as modern. Abuses are disastrously imposed as proper uses upon sincere but ill-advised efforts and the clever apostate is here and there front-paged and lionized, as usual in our country. The widely accepted prophet is rarely prophetic. Seen as heroic he is too often only the blind leading the blind. Thus the plausible expedient has become gospel and continues to be generally foisted upon those who seek better things; the conformities proclaimed by authority, however specious, temporarily mistaken for Godhead. But if they were seen for what they are worth in the realm of art as they would be seen in other realms, I am sure that the world of architecture would rise above the current abuse of the thing-mistaken-for-the-thing, to rebuke and reject these traces of simian ancestry now appearing as modern.

In every new expression of a fundamental Idea there will always be the substitutes, the imitations, dangling from it, as the soiled fringe from a good garment. It takes long years to learn that superficial commotion is habitually mistaken by our provincial society for emotion, and that motion itself — action — is dangerous: the danger ever precedent to the practice of any new essential truth. This weakness in our provincial society I have seen during the more than sixty years of my own practice of architecture: see it now none the less, perhaps exaggerated by television, radio and press. So any deeper desire for indigenous culture thus is impeded.

How, then, can it be eagerly sought by our people? A deeper hunger is needed spiritually than we seem to know. The popular desire for entertainment is exploited by the commodity merchant all down the line. In upper social brackets, as in lower, there does not seem to exist enough desire to fight exploitation by mediocrity for a more enlightened life in art but rather a disposition to succumb. Therefore beauty of thought and grace of entertainment as well as beauty of environment suffer. The culture of the spirit we so desperately need we will discover with a *new integrity* — the integrity actually necessary to preserve our civil liberties! We will learn to see what is consistent with the poetic principle in the way of daily living. If our lives are to be sacrificed let it be for a humane, more beauty-loving tomorrow: make this new age more lasting and beneficent than any lying back there in ruins ever was. We should not be looked back upon tomorrow as merely the Scientific or the Sanitary Age. This means that America must be wholeheartedly involved in the arts of town-planning and living in homes that are true works of art. This new integrity is now possible to us: as a free people we must know how to use the new sciences for genuine culture; the only genuine culture is indigenous culture.

Beautiful buildings are more than scientific. They are true organisms, spiritually conceived; works of art, using the best technology by inspiration rather than the idiosyncracies of mere taste or any averaging by the committee mind.

1902. PROJECT, DESIGN FOR CLUB HOUSE, DELAVAN LAKE, WISCONSIN

1906. UNITY TEMPLE, OAK PARK, ILLINOIS. "SO FAR AS I KNOW THE FIRST CONCRETE MONO-
LITH TO COME FROM THE FORMS AS ARCHITECTURE COMPLETELY FINISHED. THE WORK WAS
CAST IN WOODEN FORMS OR BOXES—AND THE FORMS BEAR THE IMPRESS OF THAT TECH-
NIQUE. THE PLAN FIRST BEGAN THE DESTRUCTION OF THE BOX, AND THE EMPHASIS OF IN-
TERIOR SPACE AS THE REALITY OF THE BUILDING SUBSEQUENTLY CARRIED ON. THE ENTRANCE
IS BETWEEN THE TEMPLE AND THE SECULAR ROOMS. HERE ELECTRIC LIGHTING TOOK VISIBLE
FORM IN WIRING AND BECAME A DECORATIVE FEATURE OF THE STRUCTURE."

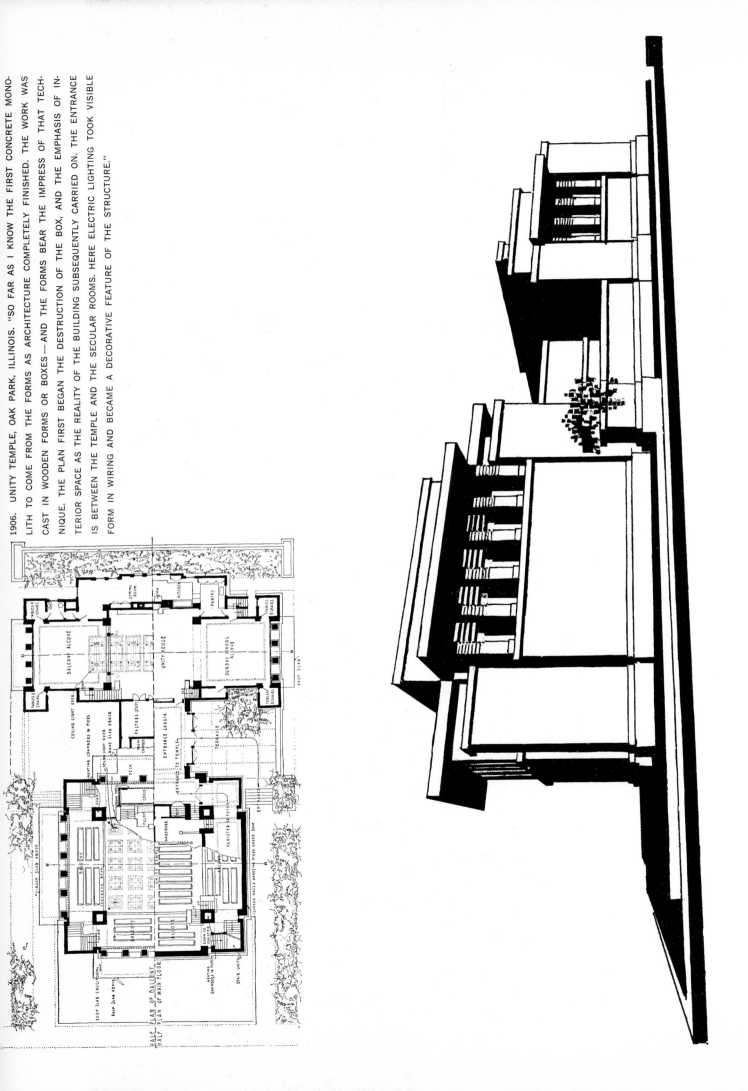

HALF PLAN OF BALCONY
HALF PLAN OF MAIN FLOOR

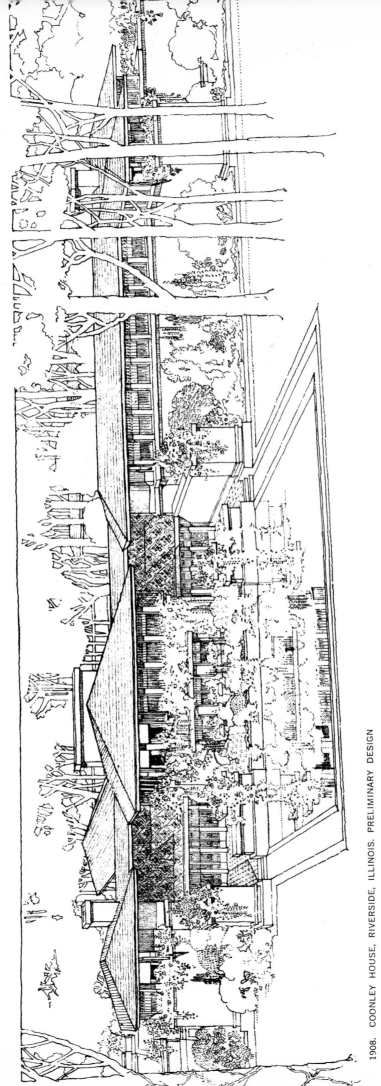

1908. COONLEY HOUSE, RIVERSIDE, ILLINOIS. PRELIMINARY DESIGN

"THE ARTICULATED PLAN—MAIN FUNCTIONS SEPARATED BY CON-
NECTING LINKS EACH INDIVIDUALIZED. MRS. COONLEY CAME TO ME
TO BUILD HER HOUSE BECAUSE SHE SAID MY 'WORK WORE THE
COUNTENANCE OF PRINCIPLE'—A GREAT ENCOURAGEMENT TO ME
AT THAT TIME."

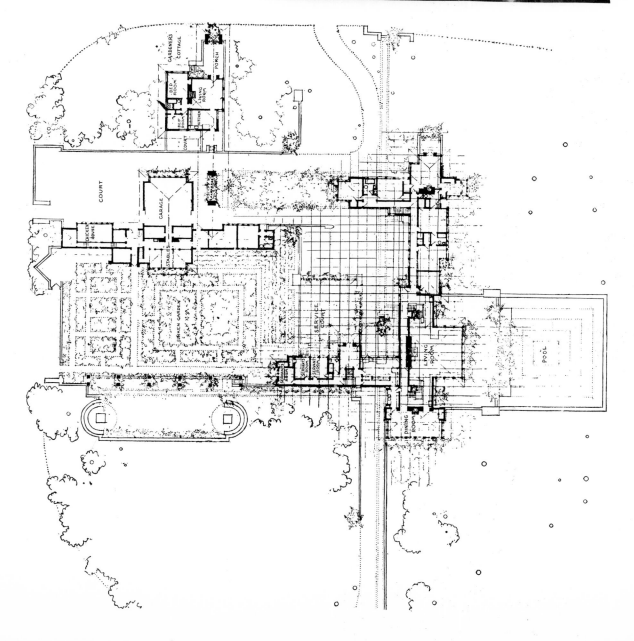

1908. COONLEY HOUSE, RIVERSIDE, ILLINOIS
GARDEN FRONT

LIVING ROOM

71

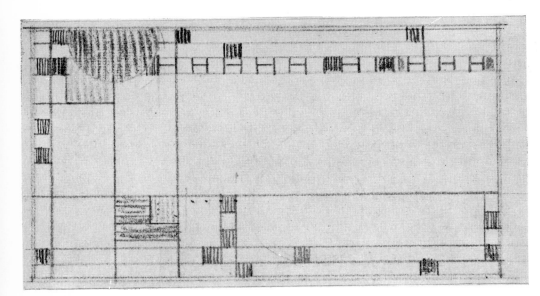

1908. PATTERNED WALL OF CERAMIC TILE
COURTYARD, COONLEY HOUSE

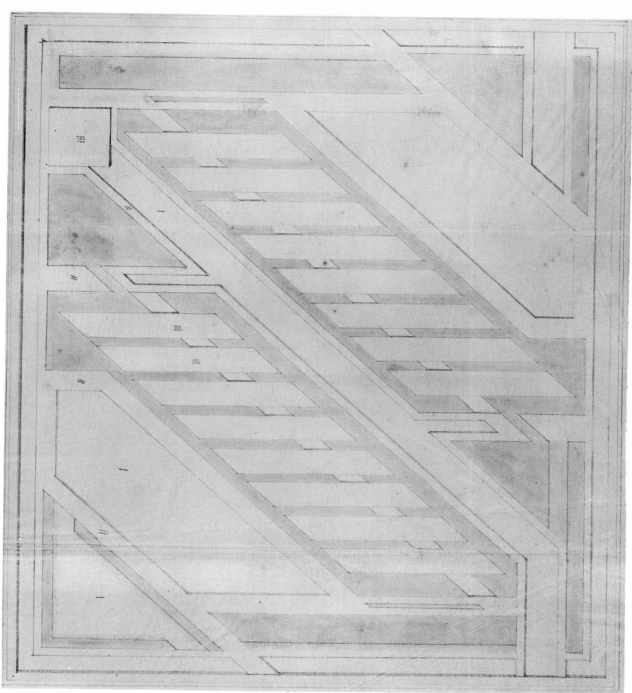

DRAWING OF CEILING SCREEN, COONLEY HOUSE

SKETCH FOR WINDOW, COONLEY STABLE

73

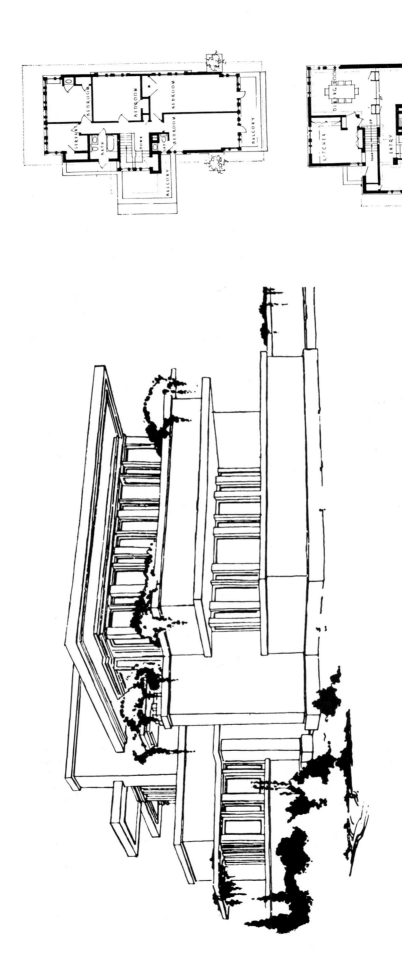

1909. GALE HOUSE, OAK PARK, ILLINOIS. MAIN FLOOR PLAN AT LOWER RIGHT — SECOND FLOOR PLAN ABOVE.

"THE GALE HOUSE BUILT IN WOOD AND PLAS-
TER IN 1909 WAS THE PROGENITOR, AS TO
GENERAL TYPE, OF FALLINGWATER, 1936."

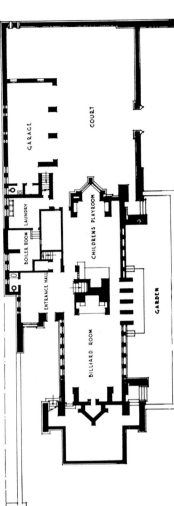

UPPER FLOOR

LOWER FLOOR

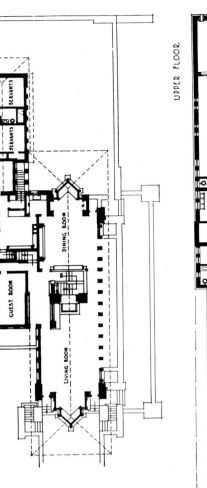

SERVANTS SERVANTS

SERVANTS

KITCHEN

GUEST ROOM

DINING ROOM

LIVING ROOM

GARAGE

COURT

BOILER ROOM LAUNDRY

ENTRANCE HALL

CHILDREN'S PLAYROOM

GARDEN

BILLIARD ROOM

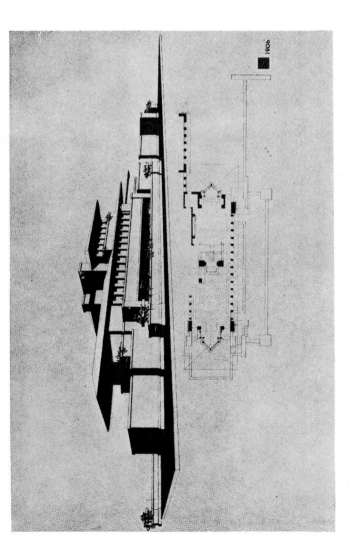

1906

1909. "THE ROBIE HOUSE, A MASONRY STRUCTURE OF TAWNY BRICK AND STONE WITH RED TILE ROOF, EAVES OF COPPER, WOODWORK OF OAK THROUGH-OUT. THIS BECAME KNOWN IN GERMANY AS DAMPFER ARCHITECTURE. IT WAS A GOOD EXAMPLE OF THE PRAIRIE HOUSE OF THAT PERIOD."

ROBIE HOUSE, CHICAGO, ILLINOIS

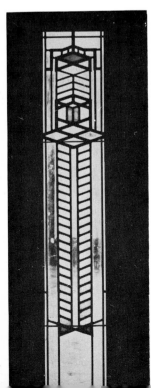

(LEFT) VIEW INTO
LIVING ROOM

(RIGHT) DETAIL,
WINDOW PATTERN

1909. ROBIE HOUSE,
CHICAGO, ILLINOIS

DETAIL, ENTRY BELOW

79

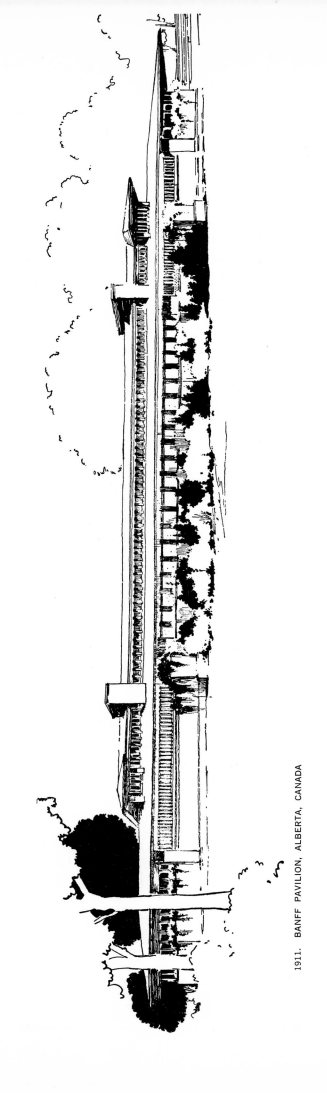

1911. BANFF PAVILION, ALBERTA, CANADA

## NEW OR OLD

Almost all our so-called "modern" is not yet new. It is merely novel by imitation or indirection; or pretense by imported picture. Our fresh architecture will be based upon nature, reinforced by the genuine democratic sentiment already existing among us as a people — a people conscious of it as the proper basis of survival as a democracy. Whether we yet know it well or not, we of this Machine-Age are growing inevitably toward organic unity not only in our architecture but in every feature of our national as well as of our private life: no *re-birth* in philosophy, art or religion for us now in any form. Birth itself.

All this as *new* is not clear enough yet, not naturally enough our social purpose. Did it so seem to our forefathers?

Why is this not more widely recognized as *natural* in the realm of education? Is it because civilization itself proceeds only by the authority of intellect and so soon becomes non-integral? Is false abstraction always the consequence of spiritual degeneration? Is decline of the spirit toward utter materialism the reason why it is so difficult for any ideal to survive? Is only the gas-pipe (materiality) safe and the lithe tendon (spirit) so difficult? Is the human nervous system now being groomed by the slaves of the expedient as a substitute for soul? If so, vital abstraction is unlikely now.

Creation is not only rare but always hazardous. Always was. But why is it growing so much more hazardous now? Is it owing to our "systems," educational and otherwise, that we seem to be capable always of less and less rather than more — less *vision* and less love essential to the understanding of exuberance? Comes to mind a triad from the old Welsh *Mabinogion* defining genius: A man who sees nature. Has a heart for nature. The courage to follow nature.

## NAISSANCE

Renaissance no longer. Comes *Naissance:* Nature. Just as Naissance has always come to the brotherhood of man at the critical moment so it came to us as a nation in the brave Declaration of principle. 1776. It has come to our architecture as the dawn of a natural free American spirit in building ourselves "into" our country, and really began about 1890. This in but one American century of civilization is dawn indeed. Thus inspired, there can be no prolonged discouragement hereafter. Many new buildings, characteristic of our own place in Time and of modern Man, have already appeared East, West, North and South. First appearing on American prairie, Midwest, they aimed to be organic and appropriate and so refused to accept, accent, or in any way serve the old forms of either European or Oriental architecture. From the start, confident, seminal, inspired by the love of architecture as well as the nature of man, notwithstanding the prevailing confusion, waste and slip by the abuse of machine-powers, the new architecture came gradually into view — in focus by 1893. A prophecy sustained.

## REVERSION

Unhappily for this early development, old-world ideas of architecture revived at the Chicago World's Fair by the professional A.I.A. had already been so firmly fixed by official and educational America that reaction was reprompted and spread countrywide over the surface of our nation. The prophecy of "Uncle Dan" already quoted, "Frank, the American people are going 'classic'" came true. European or Beaux-Arts training — old ways in architecture — were indeed "going"! Became more than ever a stumbling block. The "classic" more than ever hindered organic architecture. Even now it is confirming the robbery of our proper use of scientific invention.

## THE VIEW

Most critics of the time, as we then knew, were masters of or mastered by the odious comparison; or were inexperienced, teaching architecture by book. All were well-meaning enough but mostly made by academic armchair or managed publicity of some kind. Naturally all these agencies, though willing enough, were helpless, when deeper independent thought was urgent, especially in discriminating where architecture concerned the culture of our own society as distinguished from other societies. It has remained the blind spot of our nation. Architectural magazines were naturally more interested in architects than architecture. Architecture was not a subscriber. To them, as to the plan-factory magnate, the cliché proved a godsend. If they abandoned the one it was only to take up another. Whatever the likely cliché happened to be or wherever it came from, it was quickly salvaged by publicity and accepted, promoted and fed to the American people as the proper thing. To "the improper press" the cliché most useful in advertising and standardizing the vast fabric of our industrial and educational system was always the latest one; the names changing with stunning rapidity. But although organic architecture had already met the crushing blows of machine-age science with the right technique, not for another half-century was it to become at all operative in education. The struggle to and fro on the part of our own robust new thought, or any action based upon it, did not prevail then against the firmly established standard that "culture had to come from abroad." Suspicious always of change, established order was as usual hostile to enlightenment. So the art of building as an organism remained unfamiliar except to the more discerning, courageous, and already sentient American individual.


## BETRAYAL


As one consequence (even as a cause) architects of that period did not love architecture enough to have it on their consciences — nor did their successors. Our so-called "modern architect" lived, then as now, a curious hybrid. Gadget-lover and servile auctioneer of novelty, he was prime merchant of the common-place; speedster in all ways; quick to arrive first along the beaten path. Were he a shell-fish he would not hesitate to eat holes in his own shell. Could anything be made of *his* "housing" or *his* government's? But he has happened to us, to our country, and thrives under enormous bureaucratic expansion. Look at the sea-shell — and listen to the indictment of this hybrid.

## FAITH IN MAN

Again: mainspring of any true architecture is sound philosophy of Nature. Wherever it appears unhampered, it is the basis of the only indigenous culture yet to appear in our modern American life. The new architecture is not yet "officially" understood at home because not imported. So if not imported, as culture, not "safe"? No. No matter how sane. As for our political esthetes if they had only a glimpse of the significance of the philosophy of the new architecture, they would know it to be native. But therefore inutile or controversial. Being controversial, government would shun it. To sponsor it would not be safe for a politician because there is always "the next election." Besides since "culture has always come from abroad anyhow — why not forget the whole native thing?"

Nevertheless original organic architecture, widely recognized abroad, is now being accepted here at home although the principles upon which it stands have had little comprehension. In government, good or bad, and in education, too little of it is yet established. Gradually growing, but still puzzling or offending "arty" or routine architects and critics educated far beyond their capacity. Only among the better citizens, able to function independently of the popular effects of managed publicity or mannered art do we find the practicing architect not servile to fashion nor influenced by academic authority. Is he rare because architects have to live or because they are not sufficiently alive — and so not fit to live as architects?

## THE TROJAN HORSE—CONFIDENTIAL

Germany, 1910. After Kuno Francke's admonition at Oak Park, "Your life will be wasted here, do come to Germany," I remember Herr Dorn, major-domo of the world-famous Wasmuth Publishing House of Berlin once introduced me, when I first arrived, as "the Olbrich of America." Curiosity aroused, I went to Darmstadt to see Olbrich, only to find that the famous German architect had just passed away.

About fourteen years later, when several German architects of whom I had then not heard — Mies of the Barcelona Pavilion, Gropius of the Bauhaus, Curt

Behrendt of Prussia and, later, Erich Mendelsohn of the Einstein Turm — came over to America — I welcomed them all as sincere advocates of the battle for freedom in the dynamics of a new architecture. They knew in 1910 that I was waging a one-man war. Some twenty years or more later, it appeared that Mies (owing to Hitler's closing of the Bauhaus) was available for the post of leader at Armour Institute. The motion was seconded by me with what influence I had. Mies first arrived at Taliesin, before taking up his post in Chicago. He stayed with us there for a fortnight, speaking no English. Soon to be inducted at Armour; a banquet was given in his honor by the A.I.A. in the ballroom of the Palmer House. Mies, feeling himself a stranger, did not want to go unless I went with him.

The banquet was standard as those things go but a fulsome affair, functioning chiefly through the A.I.A. M.I.T. President Emerson read an unctuous falsification of modern architecture. Speakers of welcome, all face down to modern architecture from abroad, followed suit. All this seemed false to me and false to Mies as well. But, Mies, of course, understood nothing, sat ready to read the twenty-minute paper he had written in German at Taliesin. I was sitting next to Emerson on the raised platform where the principal speakers were gathered to honor modern architecture from abroad. Next me sat Mies. By this time I was wondering: why not let Mies speak for himself and be properly translated? But when finally his turn came I put my arm around his shoulders, led him to the podium and said, "Ladies and Gentlemen — Mies van der Rohe! Treat him well. He will reward you. He will now himself address you. He is worthy of any support you can give him. Ladies and gentlemen, I give you Mies van der Rohe." Accent on the *I*. Then, displeased, turning the podium over to Mies, I left the room, not because I did not understand German but because the whole affair had made me feel the attitude toward both Mies and myself was false; just as false to itself; another proof that modern architecture for the A.I.A. had to come from abroad. A.I.A., in one way or another, was itself from abroad — mostly Beaux-Arts à la Paris. The fact that modern architecture had been originated by a contemporary in Chicago was simply not to be borne.

Well, the twenty-minute paper Mies had prepared in his own language he proceeded to read in full, all expecting a proper translation. My friend, Ferdinand Schevill (Chair of History at Chicago University) was present. He said that

Mies' paper was to be translated by A.I.A. president Woltersdorf. Woltersdorf appeared, shuffled his feet, cleared his throat several times, looked toward President Emerson for help. Finally he said, "Ladies and gentlemen, Mr. van der Rohe says he is so sorry that Mr. Frank Lloyd Wright left so early." And that was all the assembly ever heard or will ever know of the van der Rohe acceptance speech on his American debut — unless they understood German or have since read a copy that may exist, somewhere.

Said Dr. Schevill later, "Frank, Mies van der Rohe's speech throughout was a splendid tribute to you. Obviously this was not what these A.I.A. sponsors wanted or expected. Thus — clumsily — when it appeared, they cut it out."


## CONSEQUENCES

Nevertheless the straight-line, flat-plane effects, the new shapes of shelter I had published in Germany (1910) and France (1911) have, by stimulating world-wide imitation and some true emulation, scattered far. As one consequence, temporal novelty often appears upon our urban streets; and facades more quiet than usual. They not only loom upon our urban streets, but ride our housing in countless subdivisions. But as yet, *no deep satisfaction*. This "modern-architecture" we see as a negation in two dimensions. An improvement? Yes, but with too little evidence of the depths of the architecture conceived according to Principle, built from inside outward as organism. The essence of construction itself is yet haphazard or old-fashioned steel-framing of the box. Natural elegance, the true serenity (due to indigenous character) of an organic original seems likely to be lost: sterilized by studied stylizing or by careful elimination of all ornament and pretty much all but the box-frame with a flat lid. The tranquil emphasis on space as the reality of the building is mostly missing. Parasitic practices appear everywhere, credit given to this or that new name. Always new names. But no matter how many, such derivations from the outside in all run dry. Then there are the novelty-facades that have appeared in our big cities, usually facades glassified as steel-framed boxes, often great mirrors acting as commercial posters. Fair enough! But why call this manifest advertising in the abuse of new materials, architecture? Is it possible that the City is entitled only to such negation?

Nevertheless a conscientious architect learns to understand the nature of human nature so well that the character of his structural ability may eventually justify calling organic architecture man's love of life presenting man to Man. Democracy needs this inspiration to keep democracy alive and the American people free.

Meantime pseudo-scientific minds, like those of the scientist or the painter in love with the pictorial, both teaching as they were taught to become architects, practice a kind of building which is inevitably the result of *conditioning* of the mind instead of *enlightenment*. By this standard means also, the old conformities are appearing as new but only in another guise, more insidious because they are especially convenient to the standardizations of the modernist plan-factory and wholly ignorant of anything but public expediency. So in our big cities architecture like religion is helpless under the blows of science and the crushing weight of conformity — caused to gravitate to the masquerade in our streets in the name of "modernity." Fearfully concealing lack of initial courage or fundamental preparation or present merit: reactionary. Institutional public influences calling themselves conservative are really no more than the usual political stand-patters or social lid-sitters. As a feature of our cultural life architecture takes a backward direction, becomes less truly radical as our life itself grows more sterile, more conformist. All this in order to be safe?

How soon will "we the people" awake to the fact that the philosophy of natural or intrinsic building we are here calling organic is at one with our freedom — as declared, 1776?

## THE EXPEDIENT

Circumstances I have been describing indicate lack of spiritual insight inspired by love of our own nation.

The old-time "committee-mind" is the devil's advocate in education, being justified there by the teaching of "teamwork" as safer substitute for inspiration. This justification is admission of spiritual failure. As a people we remain comparative strangers to our own life in our own time in our own home: native culture waiting in vain on our door step. Our foreign relations — nationalities abroad — seem to have inherited better perspective. Having once enjoyed a culture of their own is it easier for them to recognize indigenous culture when they see it? The peripatetic cliché, shallow by nature, is their expedient too but it cannot, there as here, wake up the average business mind in commerce; although there too, whenever this mind says *practical,* only *expedient* is meant. They say that substitutes are everywhere preferred to originals in America because originals, having more character-value and strength, are not so easily controlled and exploited as the substitute. Nor can imitation ever do more than insult original inspiration. Imitation is always insult — not flattery.

## THE SUBSTITUTE

The national recourse is the substitute, freely distributed in mutual byplay between the kind of journalese-architect, popular educator and museum-director — purveyors of the fashion — all more or less in the business of themselves — therefore all "busy" with such activity as I have described. For this, if for no other reason, degeneration of creative ability in America has had ample support, and what nobility our society might still have is in danger of being submerged in overwhelming tides of rising conformity. The artist-teacher too becomes only a conformist trader when he should by no means be either. Knowledge of principle as creative is still behind us or under foot, the uncommon slandered on suspicion and left to be revived by the youth of the future.

Meantime the multitudinous substitutes for indigenous culture cannot grow. Having no roots, they can only age and decay. Studious, sincere youth retires, defeated. American youth, capable of becoming serious competent artists, under such pressure as this on every side, confused, try not to give up — or "fall in line." This is the nature of about all that can be called American education in the arts and architecture at this time. As for religion true to the teaching of the great redeemer who said "The Kingdom of God is within *you*" — that religion is yet to come: the concept true not only for the new reality of building but for the faith we call democracy. Nevertheless and notwithstanding, I have wanted to *build* this faith — life-long.

1909.  PROJECT, LEXINGTON TERRACE, CHICAGO, ILLINOIS

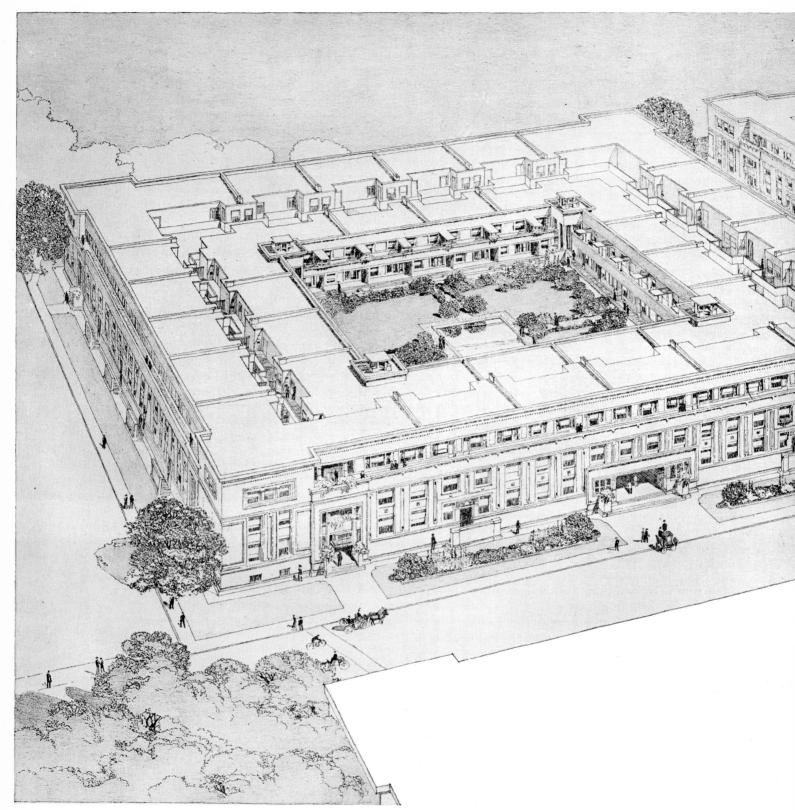

1909.   PROJECT, LEXINGTON TERRACE, CHICAGO, ILLINOIS

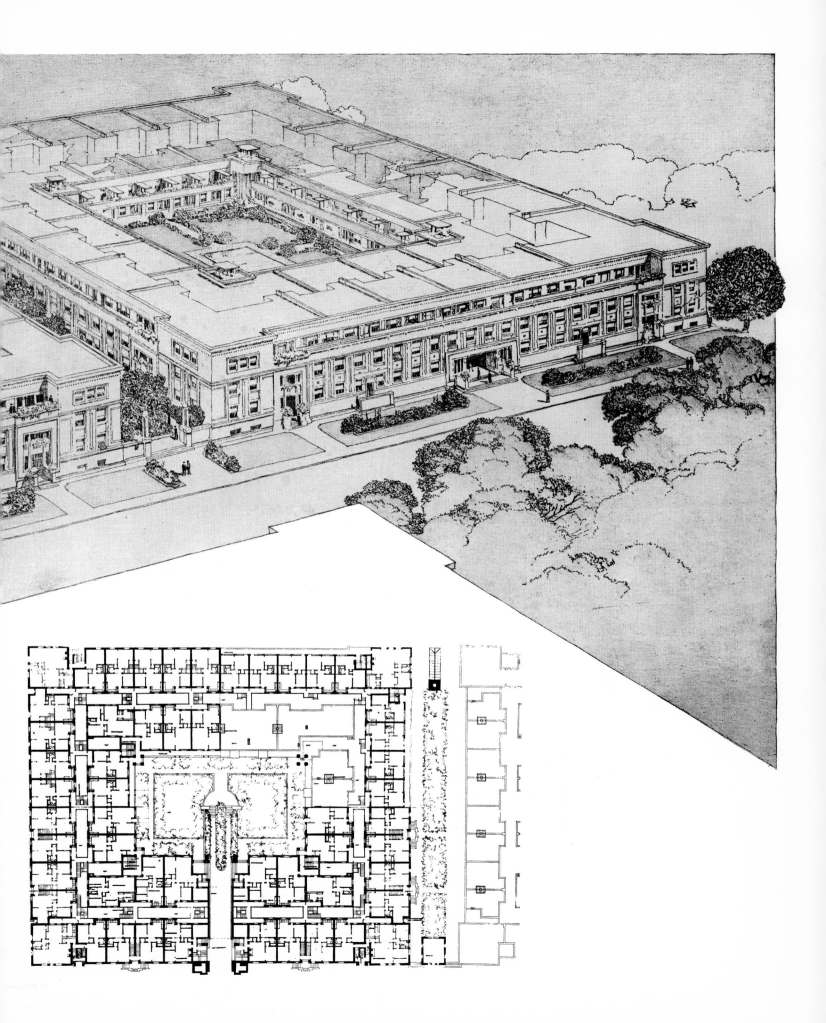

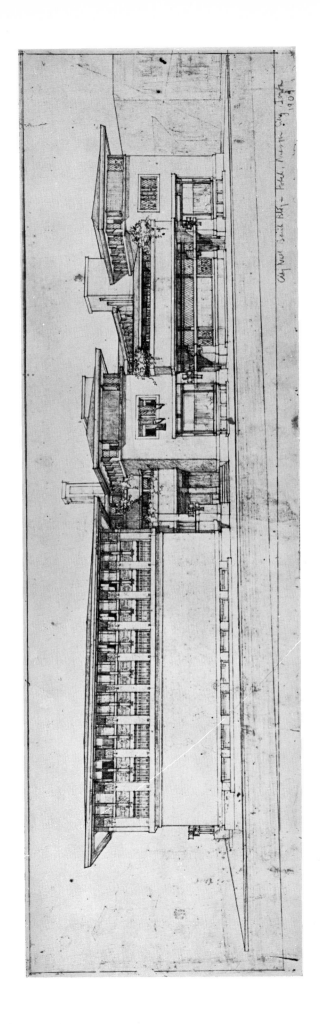

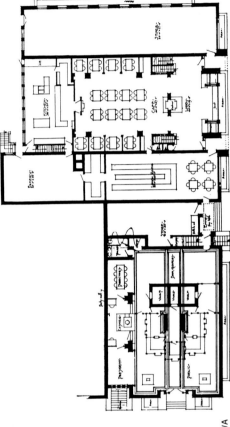

1909.  CITY NATIONAL BANK BUILDING AND HOTEL, MASON CITY, IOWA

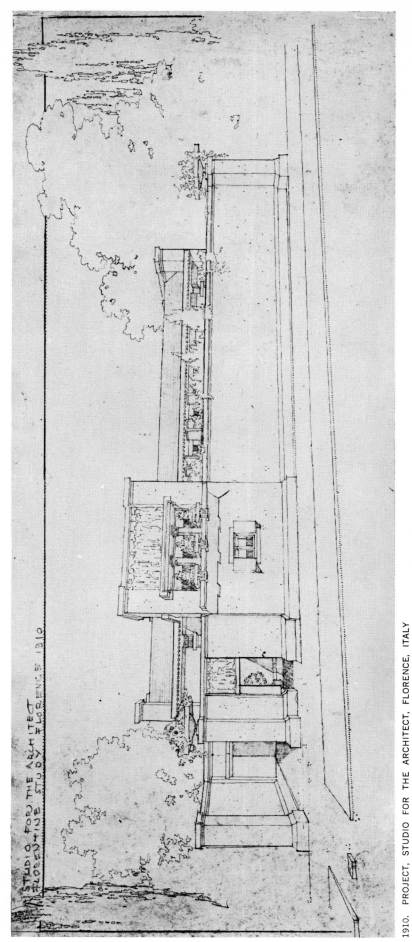

1910. PROJECT, STUDIO FOR THE ARCHITECT, FLORENCE, ITALY

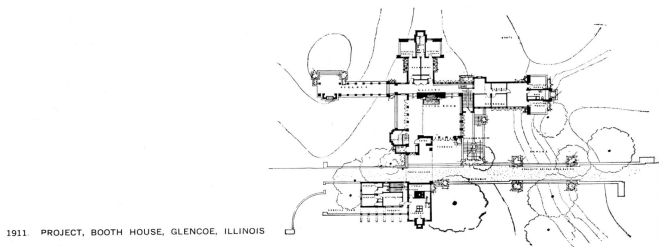

1911. PROJECT, BOOTH HOUSE, GLENCOE, ILLINOIS

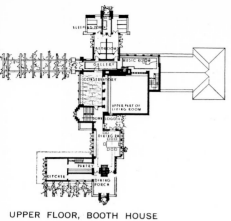

UPPER FLOOR, BOOTH HOUSE

1911. BRIDGE OVER RAVINE, GLENCOE, ILLINOIS

1912.  PROJECT, CUTTEN HOUSE,
DOWNER'S GROVE, ILLINOIS

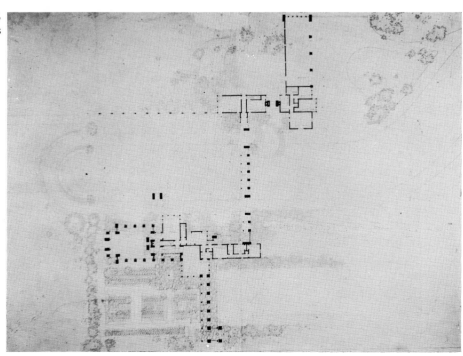

## "THE COMMON MAN"

Our schools today, busy turning out "the common man," seem to be making conformity a law of his nature. The study of architecture is often relegated to the abandoned military shed or the basement of our educational institutions, and the old adage — "those who can, *do*, those who can't, *teach*" — was never more truly descriptive of purveyors of "the higher education" in architecture. Life-long I have been shocked by the human deficiency capitalized by American education.

Many of our young men are eager, groping; hopeful that our civilization, now over a century and a half old, may still wholeheartedly desire indigenous culture and enable the fundamental distinctions between art creative, science inventive and taste intuitive to be learned by schooling. But they are fed prejudicial comparisons instead of the results of patient intelligent analyses or performance based upon nature-study encouraged. Forced to choose this or that personality, they must give up trying to find their direction within themselves, their powers of interior analysis weakened and confused by stock comparisons. Comparisons made by whom? By those who themselves have been bred upon similar comparisons — all odious. No wonder that persistent analysis based upon actual experience is so rare.

Also, "Truth told with bad intent beats all the lies man can invent."* Truth faces this travesty today.

This is no exaggerated indictment of our nationwide neglect of basic experience and principle as a qualification. Regents, curators, professors and critics, with too few exceptions seem paid to honor by comparison — still unable to go deeper into the vital nature of art. Should our life be either ready-made or made to the measure of this conformity, by casual journalese or the prophets of the profit system? Why should it be essentially influenced by such personal opinion as our critics and museums seek to inflict? The answer seems to be that education has not learned to draw with firm, courageous hand the dividing line

_____
* William Blake.

between the merely Curious and the truly Beautiful; and knows culture only by rote or hearsay or taste. Science may easily mistake the curious for the beautiful and often does, instinctively preferring the curious. For evidence we need only go to the buildings in which scientific education unwittingly administers paralysis of the sense of beauty to the optic nerve. This fatal defect in "the higher learning" is tragic and can only beget servility to our "catch-as-catch-can" culture. Reform only means more conformity. It is form first that is needed. And it is not to be found in sporadic endeavors to remodel our lives by imported aesthetics — even if we import our own export. We will not be able to maintain faith in democracy merely by profit-system equipment, nor help it grow by the conditioning our youngsters receive in the name of education.

## THE NEED FOR THE NEW AMERICAN

New enlightenment and courage is needed to help resist such influences. The soul of any civilization on earth has ever been and still is Art and Religion, but neither has ever been found in commerce, in government or the police. We cannot long console ourselves with the thought that we are at the mercy of a numerical materialism. Votes are counted. Yes — but vision can neither be counted nor discounted.

Our good hope lies in the hearts of men and women of vision rather than in the minds habituated by such education as we now provide. Democracy's best hope for survival lies in, let's say, the upper middle third of our American families — the better units of our present society. In the communications we at Taliesin receive daily from students in the high schools of the nation, I see teenage interest in architecture already evident there: Dynamic spiritual force, parallel to the spirit of our democracy itself — when not pushed too far scienceward or arrested by conformity; or when not too sentimentally inclined by parental sense of tradition or confused by the categorical-imperative in art — is now organic and therefore poetic. Art expression is by nature romantic; and this awakening interest cannot long survive without a sound philosophy to give it direction and true religion to give it emotion. Both Art and Religion are on the way. Both must go hand in hand as ever before. Both together illuminating our sciences will constitute the soul of this civilization.

## MAN ABOVE LAW OR LAW ABOVE MAN

By attempts to keep man-made law alive when by nature it is dead, the spirit in which law was made is betrayed and so is law. My father taught me that a law is originally made to prevent or cure some timely, manifest evil; the law usually made by "experts." (An expert? Generally, a man who has stopped thinking because he knows!) So whenever court judgments continue to be based upon "the letter of the law," long after the good intended by the letter goes out of it, judges defy its sense and betray justice. The law, whenever (too often) put above man, ceases to shed the light of reason. Justice then becomes, not true servant of the humanities, but mere routine; and so we fail of democracy, robbed of our title to manhood. Again, the calamitous drift toward conformity. Again, fear instead of reverence for life as hoped by our forefathers. Again, "bigness" legally engendered — by standardizing human beings into "the common man."

Yes, and because the "common" man is a man who believes only in what he sees and sees only what he can put his hand on, he — the hero of "all men are created equal but some are more equal than others" — is by lack of vision made to become a caricature of himself.

Do not call this exploitation of massology — Democracy. Mobocracy is the more proper term: When any man is compelled to sign away his sovereignty as an individual to some form of legalized pressure by government or society or to some kind of authorized gangsterism democracy is in danger of sinking to communism. This shall not be our fate.

## WALT WHITMAN — SEER OF DEMOCRACY

When Walt Whitman, asked for the cure for evils of Democracy, replied, "more Democracy," for us he touched a great truth. But patriotism can eventually become "the last refuge of the scoundrel." What did our poet of democracy mean by *democracy?*

The terms of democratic salvation may only be found deep within man himself by his comprehension of the basic principles of nature and of his own human nature. Then — without popular prejudice, sentimentality or fear — we will achieve the native culture we can *honestly call our own.* We will reach the expressions of our own democratic nature by probing the depths to discover our one-ness. More important than war or "segregation" is this original idea of "integration"? Integration that lies implicit in life as in art, architecture and natural religion.

## BEGINNING

Back to the Froebel kindergarten-table. Presented by my teacher-mother with the Froebel "gifts," then actually as a child I began to be an architect; unless long before, when I chose my ancestors with the greatest care. So this son of a teacher-mother and a musician preacher-father grew up blissfully unaware of worldly conflicts in our brave experiment in human liberation, as here presented. Many years later when I had grown up and began to practice architecture it was in time to become keenly aware, perhaps too zealous, where the social situation I have been trying to describe was a concern; thus earning the epithet "arrogant."

Looking backward now: When I put the gold letters "Frank Lloyd Wright Architect" on the plate-glass panel of my office door in "The Schiller," 1893, the causes of the cultural lag I encountered lay in the social bias created by growing eclecticisms in the practices of the A.I.A. Dead-sea fruit of inadequate architectural education. The true character of American life was being submerged.

Nevertheless — rather more — owing to this social confusion of ethics in our ways and means, there was growing up native strength enough to keep faith with this vision of the new birth in art and architecture, the awakening prophesied by the great French poet: first made imperative by the American Declaration and Constitution. We have come thus far to see the end, forever, of "restatement" as creative art. We know that the beginning of all true significance in great art must be not only appropriate but parallel in philosophy to our faith in man. The fundamental new freedom in architecture was on record about 1893; the new philosophy in architecture came to parallel in art what had been so bravely asserted by the original statesmanship of 1776. American architecture confirmed the prophecy of Victor Hugo by becoming action; beginning to feel sinews anew, take on vital flesh, lift its head high for new vision. New forms were born — forms natural to freedom! Shapes in building, unfamiliar but peculiar to the modern circumstances of machine-technique, were then evolving. Engineering advances by adventure in new machine-age materials and techniques began to be natural and many of these are to be seen in the illustrations herewith. For the first time, then, new straight-line, flat-plane, "streamlined" designs, adapted to machine uses, became more or less familiar as technique to architects (imitations of these effects you may buy today as a cliché from the plan factories). These new effects were born with a new sense of integrity. They were not unbecoming nor devoid of human grace. Call that grace: ornament. Even though a disgrace, machine-made, ornament stayed and still thrives.

But no sincere help for "the new reality" was found in any authoritarian body, either Beaux-Arts or A.I.A. No jealousy is comparable to professional jealousy, so this trait was to be expected by the new architecture to say nothing of a new architect. So the New by sheer force of character was compelled to break through neglect and barriers continually arising and due to private and public indifference, animosity or fear — the dominant characteristics of "culturists," promoted and patronized by machine-masters, themselves becoming merchandisers of "the Past." Our tradition was the inexorable Past. As regents and leaders, these would-be bulwarks of tradition had and still have ownership in the realm of education. Worthless traditions were "safe." Ideas not utterly archaic but traditional were alone respectable. This graft upon the future still called conservatism. As a matter of fact our social register itself was then not much above a market record. Family and especially official society, if unconsciously, made merchandise of itself. All purblind cultures were thus on sale, our "57 varieties" were made available by the A.I.A. itself to the elite who kept on buying by taste — and regardless.

Thus culture at the time I was entering the practice of architecture seemed to be hopelessly involved with making a living. It was this mongrelized affair which had never learned the values of native beauty or even realized the virtues of original beauty. The meretricious substitute everywhere: the elite, enthusiastically all looting "from abroad," were scavengers in the name of "refinement." William Randolph Hearst was perhaps ideal exemplar in this class though he had powerful competition. American wealth quite generally founded "modern" museums, and art institutes were dedicated as educational enterprises to this or that; town libraries all over the country were thrown in. An amazing mass of perfectly good material was to be found there, all wrong in the right places or right in the wrong places. Too many of these public benefactors were simply buying tickets for a preferred or at least a respectable place as a reward for these virtues to be conferred in the hereafter?

Reading here like merely a sordid old-wives' tale, this dreary addiction to excess by American success was really a teeming hive characterized by will, speed, ruthless competition, contradiction and fury but always action, getting the unintended insult to the fore with amazing hindsight. For my part, by this time on my own, the master (L.H.S.) gone — I faced this tantalizing and threatening challenge to what I stood for: the end of which is not yet seen — if ever? Can co-existence be effected between body and soul by science? No. By art and religion? Yes, together with science. I am bound to think that we in America have the answer in the principles of building called organic architecture.

## INSIDE OUT—OUTSIDE IN

In order to become national reality, this intrinsic philosophy (new and yet so ancient) now interior to the competent architect as man or creative artist, must, so I see, destroy any cultural or educational fetish whatsoever; especially destroy the fetish of "a style," a cliché.


Yet to come to modern architecture, as official, in this world is *Style* as style for its own sake. But never — now — should we in America be caught in the fetters or the talons of *a* style. Certainly not, when natural building is free to live from within outward with our magnificent new equipment. Already the Idea is again vital and fascinating. The triumph of spirit over circumstance is evident nation-wide. This expression of idea if genuine has always had style and so always sure of popular appeal. "Style" is becoming an American "natural."

PART TWO

# FORM—A BIRTH

Again to architecture comes the serenity of the right idea; human integrity is in action. True significance of line, color and form is now the very method of construction. Principle itself is looking out from our American habit of thinking about planning not only buildings but planning the new city; developing this beauty in our villages by appropriate uses of ground: learning now how to build and dwell in a building as a work of art: dwell harmonious with our own Time, Place and Man. We need be apostate no longer. Now we are apotheosis, able to master our vast facilities of machine power and the sciences.

New methods and new means continue to arrive. Well-adapted forms may be seen based upon Principle instead of Precedent! Instead of the incongruous selecticisms, ambiguous forms of a dated aristocracy, forged by illegitimate taste upon the legitimate patterns of machine craft, here come the concepts of genuine forms to rescue character from ruin by false leadership or any hangover from the Renaissance: perhaps rescue America itself from recession? Our era is still young, yet more or less nostalgic, so Victorian in spite of our progress. The motorcar is yet a wagon trying to digest four wheels when ruts no longer exist. Etc. But Ruskin and Morris are now "once upon a time." Going and gone also are the ites and all isms of the modernistic. The rational is no longer inimical to art and architecture or the reverse. The spirit may live anew.

## NEW PHILOSOPHY

This philosophy of organic character develops new strength; timely apprehensions going deeper (and wider); penetration into the heart of "matter"; the true nature of a new building-construction is now indigenous. When understood as a principle it applies to architecture anywhere on earth. The great mother-art, Architecture, is still living. Never in history has timely philosophy asserted itself in action more quietly or simply. Witness, here, Unity Temple, the Taliesins, the Hillside Home School and the Larkin Building. Amidst turbulent changes a way of building has brought to our society a new integrity. Principle recognized despite our hectic superficiality. Integrity has been proved feasible in actual practice. These simple buildings themselves show architecture to be *organism*, based upon: "part is to part as part is to whole." Only such entity can live. Inevitably this nature-concept was individual in architecture as it was individual in the Declaration of Independence and characteristic of the nature of man himself. Wholeness of humane expression in architecture is now assured. Never again could successful building be otherwise. "Such as the life is, such is the form."*

Poets, Jesus and Laotze leading them, have so declared from time to time. Poets the "unacknowledged legislators of the world"; preservers of the human race. Laotze expressed this truth, now achieved in architecture, when he declared the "reality of the building does not consist in the roof and walls but in the space within to be lived in." I have built it. When Unity Temple was built this sense of interior space began to "come through": 1906.


## NEW INTEGRITY

To Americans thus came natural, free building. For mankind *the ideal* of man free, therefore his own building humanistic. Both these freedoms I understood then as now to be basic to all our modern art, parallel to the *idea* by which we live and have our being as a people. This is the meaning of democracy. Architecture will never long be satisfied by the shell itself nor by anything done

---

* Samuel Coleridge

to it in the name of Architecture. It will now be conceived only as integral feature of Interior Space. Because of this more humane sense of cultural integrity by this new way of building, entity is born to put an end to mere machine-age depravity in our culture. This new ideal to shape appropriate environment for life — free — is now true determinant of technology and no less of style!

## PRINCIPLE BEFORE PRECEDENT

Here then is new "school." Principle-before-Precedent. Negation of the national current of haphazard, standby, knockdown taste: new basis for all kinds of aesthetic or ethical achievement. A new "school" able to turn right side up almost all perversions by modern*ism*, enabling the architect forever to prevent the return of classicism. Struggle for natural performance in American architecture begun all over again. To continue . . . how long?

In any case liberal in thought means liberal in art. The nineteenth century has given birth to new achievement: comes in time to be in tune with the awakening prophesied "late in the nineteenth century or early in the twentieth . . ." Now comes a twentieth-century architecture. The mother-art of civilization should be able to live no longer tied down by formalistic fashioning nor be put into harness or into uniform either by academic education or political authority; be further stultified by science or vulgarized by commercial success. Our human environment may now be conceived and executed *according to nature*: the nature of Time, Place and Man: native as was always natural to cultures wherever life in the past was strongest, richest and best. The level always highest when *native*.

This upshoot of indigenous art is already dedicated to our democracy: alive none too soon, organic expression of modern life square with our forefathers' faith in man as Man. Sovereignty of the individual now stems true as the core of indigenous culture in the arts and architecture. Yet to come to us as a free people is the organic *religion* natural to this new era of organic faith in man. Organic economy would naturally follow. Sovereignty in this sense of a new religion is needed to go hand in hand with man truly free. Human sensibilities, little by little, are opening to vistas of the new America.

## "NORMALCY"

The more any building as Idea is true to the Idea itself the better I like the building. The more it is likely to be in itself a free wholeness of expression of the Idea. It stands then for the ideal building that would be wholesome as a work of art. And the more the home is a work of art in our society now the better even for the selfish property instincts of the owner.

What is called "efficiency" among us is to be regarded with suspicion, or impatience, because it has too little sympathy with the deficiency that now goes with it. The alcoholic, the chain-smoker or habituate in any form has, for me, a claim upon pity too strong to be borne. I have always regarded him with wonder or suspicion. So to be a doctor was not an ambition of mine. I believed that all was possible if in full accord with nature. I believed that less than this was the result of either poverty or sin.

So I have grown up intolerant of any "falling short" by way of pretense, artificiality, limitations or scholasticism or of any form of brainwashing. Insufficiency of any sort becomes increasingly the mortgage on freedom. Mercy is a divine quality, and always somewhere as a quality of my soul, but too often severely "strained." If mercy was spontaneous (genuine) I loved the quality of mercy, perhaps most of all, divine. But I have always hated "efficiency" *per se,* as I see it standardized in American life in big or little business. No less hate it in daily life as the "E Pluribus Unum" of success. Life thus over-organized is always deficient, soon becomes a form of imposition.

What I am trying to say is that life is fullness of love when *normal to the human being* and it is so either in the realm of ideas or in the nature of building

— or conduct. Body, if used as and when *guided by spirit,* constitutes man's true virtue and the quality that distinguishes him from the brute. Exuberance has always seemed to me constituent good health. Poverty of any kind I view with deep dread as a kind of punishment flourishing upon deprivation. Exuberance to me early meant ecstacy of love, the poetic principle of life. Therefore, Beauty, as the poet Blake said it was. In this sense I have loved life with pertinacity and delight in ever new phases of idealization — in which love itself is realization. These eternal springs of inspiration never run dry for the human spirit in love with Nature's exuberance. Through lack of this life-given exuberance, love from within, the fountain-head of Art goes dry.

The "classic" was excess negation by rote: dry. The Renaissance became a dry tree. The "tree dry" was William Morris' withering symbol for jealousy or hatred. To this day it is so to me. Nature's own inexhaustible fertility is manifest exuberance, and never less than the elemental poetry of all her structure. So it will be in the structure of all our native culture when we do arrive at a culture of our own. The love we know as beauty and the beauty we know as love will be natural to our civilization and no longer will every prospect please while man alone is vile. I propose as the symbol of this love — the tree.

## THE NATURE OF NATURE

I would here again eliminate confusion too often caused by my use of the word "nature." So many years ago when I began to write and speak upon the subject of architecture I used the word to mean "the interior essence of all cause and effect." My sense of "native" thus took the inner nature of the poetic principle to be right in whatever it might consist or make manifest. *Truth,* this was, of any object or condition: this was to me the innate sense of *origin.* The original.

According to my training at my mother's kindergarten table this was the activating *cause* of all visible effects. Nor, later, was it necessarily moral, but always ethical. For instance, the essence of a brick, of course, lies in its brickness. In a machine it lies in its dependable mechanism. The same of a human heart, a sinew or a screw or any interior activating impulse or synthesis; parts whether of a pump, a brook, a stone; sex, a scoundrel or a poem. All this became inexorable thesis of man as a whole. Innate sense of scale then was proportion. Really investiture of life in our present time — not to be distinguished from all time? I have continually asked myself this question. What is the great or small difference between "then and now?"

What is this life of ours today; is man in his new place in Time? What kind of Man is this man of today? What of his civilization? Nature is how now? What is Man as he is? Where does this activation of life-force apply to old or new form, and what is substance as he represents it to be God or Devil? What lies ahead of us all now as we wander confused in the capacious lap of Change? Are we really helpless as we seem? What would be the nature of the abstraction that could be intelligently made to clarify and defend us in what we are calling "civilization"? In short, in what does man really consist as he exists in our native civilization?

The answer to all such questions lies implicit in human Nature. I have always wanted to build for the man of today, build his tomorrow in, organic to his own Time and his Place as modern Man. Therefore come these questions about *him*. And what is Art, now? What countenance would his life on earth really wear if not spurious or on masquerade? Of course it should be expression of his spirit and natural to his circumstances. Is it? Now, what Architecture would be *natural* to him? Can any man maintain this prevalent divorce from nature under the new freedom? But is man yet capable to live as the world's "free man"? Would he be capable of *anything* natural as things are with him? For so long has his excitable nervous system been his substitute for soul — how much is left of his soul now? Has modern man, by his taste for sensation and desire for security, become prone to mere expediency? Can his education, too long fashioned upon his expediency, be more than a false moment in history? Has false environment already made him a mere numerical factor, trampling with the herd? Is this atmosphere of ugliness he now endures actually created by him without his knowing it to be the result of his own confusion of mind? Or his impotence? He has lived so long subject to conformity or conflict that his judgment is atrophied? Has his habit of servility to custom and circumstance becomes servitude to mediocrity? Or is it that he fears his taste for the "unusual" might shut him in or shuttle him back again to insecurity? (There is nothing so timid as a million dollars.) Why does my brother live as a mendicant in this servility he thus puts upon himself or is put upon him because he puts it upon others? What is this modern man's true nature? Is something deadly put upon him by his false sense of himself extended to others? By being so far educated beyond his capacity is he unable to learn within himself from Nature? Divorced as he is from her, who and what can now be his? Does the so-called free man of democracy merely exploit his sovereignty?

Let us look back. I remember how as a boy, primitive American architecture — Toltec, Aztec, Mayan, Inca — stirred my wonder, excited my wishful admiration. I wished I might someday have money enough to go to Mexico, Guatemala and Peru to join in excavating those long slumbering remains of lost cultures; mighty, primitive abstractions of man's nature — ancient arts of the Mayan, the Inca, the Toltec. Those great American abstractions were all earth-architectures: gigantic masses of masonry raised up on great stone-paved terrain, all planned as one mountain, one vast plateau lying there or made into the great mountain ranges themselves; those vast areas of paved earth walled in by stone construction. These were human creations, cosmic as sun, moon, and stars! Nature? Yes, but the nature of the human being as he was, then. *Entity even more cosmic* had not yet been born. The machine then was but a simple lever in the hand of the slave: man himself a menial, subject to the cruel despotisms of high authority; priests imposing "divine" mysteries upon his lack of a better sense of himself. This he called "divinity" by equally mysterious authority. By the will of despots his hands were thus tied behind his back. He was himself but an obedient tool. His magnificent masonry was architecture beyond conceivable human need; truly monumental. Monuments to the gods of temporal power were laid out and built upon the great man-made stone-paved earth-levels of South American plateau. Architectural grandeur was thus made one with the surrounding features of mountainous land; made by wasting away the mountains; mountains moved at will by the simple persistent might of the human being multiplied, a man's own strength multiplied by the strength of multitudes of his kind. By such direct and simple multiplication of strength his buildings grew to be man-mountains. All were built as and for grandiloquent religious rituals to stand forever in the eye of the sun as the earthly embodiment of the mystery of human majesty, honoring deity. Thus man was made into, built into, living harmony with surrounding mountains by the physical might of primitive man. Reverence for authority was thus made manifest and mighty by the nature of manpower thus animated. All this great, man-building took place with a splendid human sense of primitive resources and the majesty of what was then apprehended as Man's place in Nature. All was exponent of great nature and, as we have called civilization, an abstraction. There was architecture by powerful primitive manpower. Basic it was, but based upon glorified abnegation of man to authority because of what he himself did not know. Such was his worship. His sense of beauty as a mighty son of Earth! Man's God involved with the worship of means to ends then — as now? A grandeur arose in the scale of total building never since excelled, seldom equalled by man either in truth of plan or simple primitive integrity of form. Architecture intrinsic to Time, Place and Man.

## NOW—FREEDOM IS FROM WITHIN

But now the man, potent lever of primitive authority in architecture, has been given even more powerful means with which to build. The science of the Machine. Already a power grown to dominant world-power. Worship of this power has grown by means of the man of science. But science in true human civilization is but a tool. Science is inventive but creative never.

So many centuries later, American man begins to build again. Something has happened to his buildings. Notwithstanding his new sciences, nor due to them, a more powerful vision has come to him, the higher sense of his own soul. This is his own sovereignty — his freedom as native American. Interior vision far greater now even in grandeur of construction, himself therefore more deeply creative as an individual, there comes to him this concept of "might" as spiritual. The dignity and worth to himself of the soul of individual man — a man no longer a tool of power or of a monarch or of any exterior authority, a man not

1912.  PROJECT, SMALL TOWN HOUSE

FIRST SKETCH OF MIDWAY GARDENS 1913

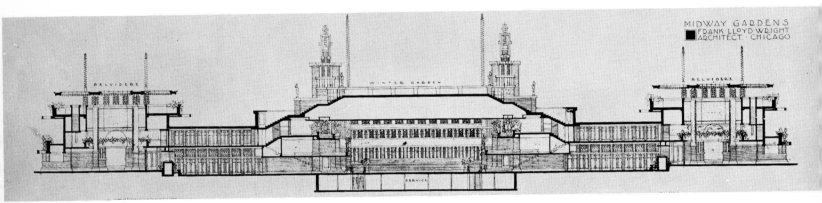

MIDWAY GARDENS
FRANK·LLOYD·WRIGHT
ARCHITECT·CHICAGO

CROSS SECTION

MIDWAY GARDENS
FRANK·LLOYD·WRIGHT
ARCHITECT·CHICAGO

NORTH ELEVATION

114

1913-14. THE MIDWAY GARDENS, CHICAGO, ILLINOIS.
AN EARLY ATTEMPT TO CORRELATE ARCHITECTURE, MUSIC,
SCULPTURE AND PAINTING IN A GREAT GARDEN SIMILAR
TO THE BEER GARDENS OF GERMANY.

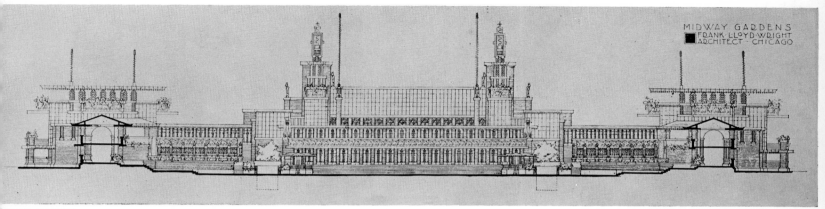

CROSS SECTION

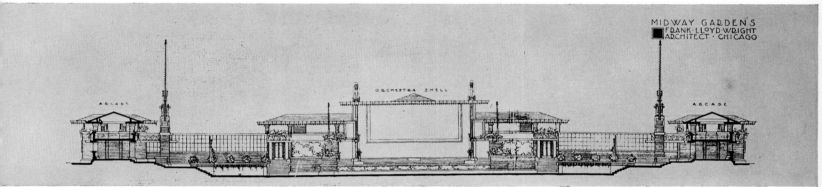

CROSS SECTION

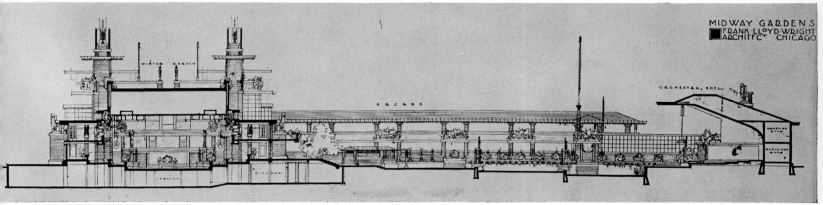

LONGITUDINAL SECTION

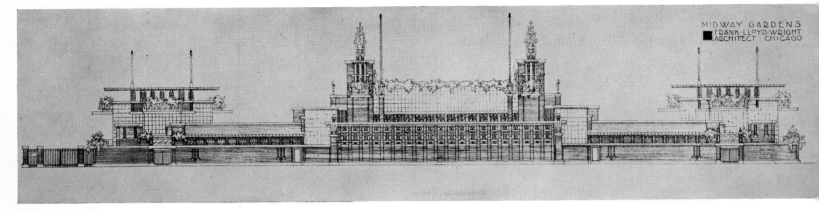

EAST ELEVATION

1913-14. THE MIDWAY GARDENS, CHICAGO, ILLINOIS. THE ENTIRE
PLACE WAS REINFORCED CONCRETE AND TAN COLORED BRICK.

1913-14.  THE MIDWAY GARDENS, CHICAGO, ILLINOIS. THE STRUCTURE WAS SO SOL-
IDLY BUILT THAT SUBSEQUENTLY, WHEN PROHIBITION CAME, IT COST SO MUCH TO
TEAR DOWN THAT SEVERAL CONTRACTORS WERE BANKRUPTED BY THE ATTEMPT.

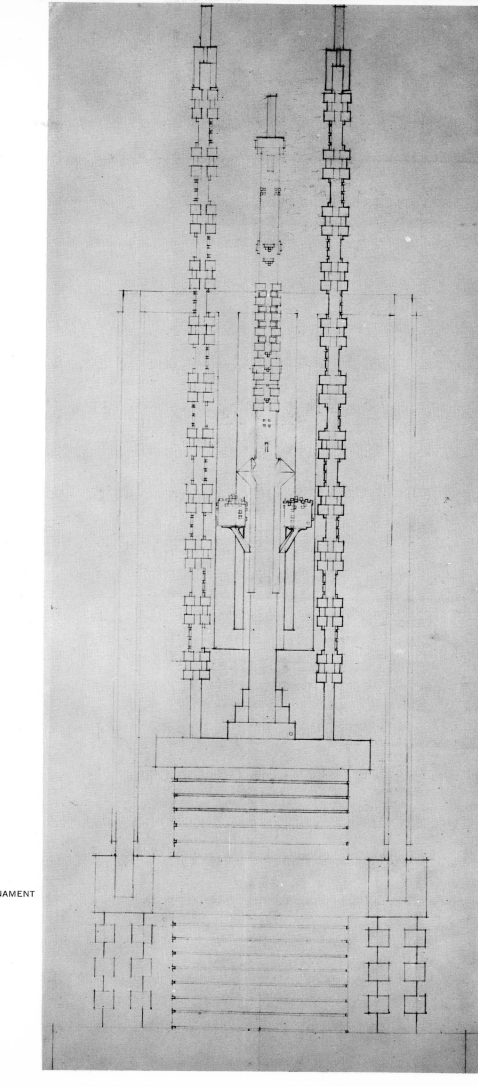

MACHINE-AGE ORNAMENT

1913-14. THE MIDWAY GARDENS, CHICAGO, ILLINOIS

"THE MURALS AND THE SCULPTURE WERE ALL INTEGRAL WITH THE ARCHITECTURE, THE ORCHES-
TRAL SHELL A GREAT SUCCESS ACOUSTICALLY, ASTONISHING EVERYONE EXCEPT THE ARCHITECT."

1915.   PROJECT. AMERICAN SYSTEM READY-CUT DUPLEX FLATS.

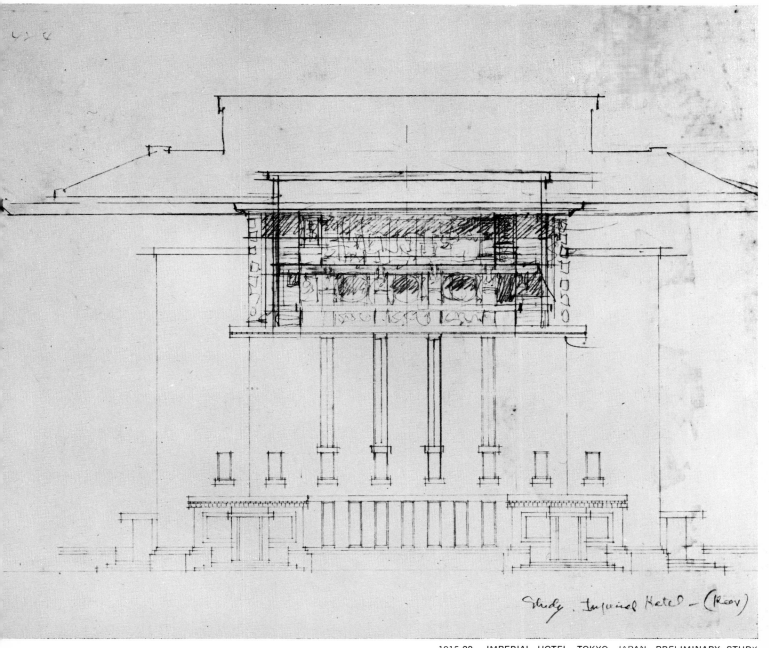

Study, Imperial Hotel — (Rear)

1915-22. IMPERIAL HOTEL, TOKYO, JAPAN. PRELIMINARY STUDY

"THE IMPERIAL HOTEL, BUILT FOR THE ROYAL HOUSEHOLD OF JAPAN, WAS A TRIBUTE TO JAPAN AS SHE WAS RISING FROM HER KNEES TO HER FEET. SHE HAD BEEN EATING FROM THE FLOOR, SLEEPING ON THE FLOOR, AND NOW HAD TO LEARN TO SIT AT TABLES AND CLIMB INTO BED TO SLEEP. THE BUILDING WAS INTENDED TO HARMONIZE WITH THOSE AROUND THE MOAT ACROSS THE PARK BEFORE IT. THE ROYAL HOUSEHOLD WAS SHOCKED WHEN I DECIDED TO USE OYA, THE STONE-ORDINAIRE UNDER FOOT IN TOKYO FOR THE STRUCTURE, WITH A BRICK HANDMADE IN JAPAN FOR THE FIRST TIME. THE ARCHITECT PERSEVERED, FINALLY GOT WHAT HE WANTED, AND GREAT BLOCKS OF OYA BEGAN FLOATING DOWN BY SEA AND CANAL FROM THE QUARRIES OF NIKKO TO THE SITE. BUT A PERMIT TO BUILD THE BUILDING WAS AWAITED IN VAIN. FINALLY A MEETING WITH THE AUTHORITIES WAS HELD AT WHICH THEY TOOK THE VIEW THAT A WORLD FAMOUS ARCHITECT WOULD NOT COME TO JAPAN TO BUILD SOMETHING THAT WOULD FALL DOWN UNDER ANY CIRCUMSTANCES. THEY COULD NOT UNDERSTAND THE PROPOSITIONS WE MADE BUT WERE WILLING TO WATCH AND WAIT AND PROBABLY LEARN SOMETHING WORTH LEARNING. ACCORDINGLY WE PROCEEDED — TO BUILD THE BUILDING WITH ALL THE HELP THEY COULD GIVE.

"I HAVE SOMETIMES BEEN ASKED WHY I DID NOT MAKE THE OPUS MORE 'MODERN.' THE ANSWER IS THAT THERE WAS A TRA-DITION THERE WORTHY OF RESPECT AND I FELT IT MY DUTY AS WELL AS MY PRIVILEGE TO MAKE THE BUILDING BELONG TO THEM SO FAR AS I MIGHT. THE PRINCIPLE OF FLEXIBILITY INSTEAD OF RIGIDITY HERE VINDICATED ITSELF WITH INSPIRING RESULTS. BUT THE A.I.A. COMMISSION SENT TO STUDY CONDITIONS IN JAPAN SUBSEQUENT TO THE GREAT TEMBLOR OF 1922 MADE NO MENTION OF THE STRUCTURE."

1915-22.   IMPERIAL HOTEL, TOKYO, JAPAN

EMPEROR'S ENTRANCE

1915-22.   IMPERIAL HOTEL, TOKYO, JAPAN. GARDEN COURT

BANQUET HALL
AND BALLROOM

1917.  PROJECT: ODAWARA HOTEL, NAGOYA, JAPAN

1921.  SKETCH, JIYU GAKUEN SCHOOL, TOKYO, JAPAN

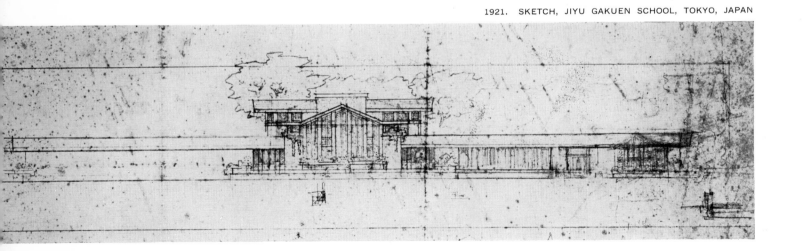

bowed down to sacrificial mysticism but man free. Kingship now of his own soul ruled by conscience and increasingly cultured intelligence. This man has risen: himself gradually coming awake to power even greater than man's primitive power because it is power of the spirit. A new ideal of civilization arises based upon freedom of man's mind guided by his conscience. In view of this new abstraction the past subsides. Ever higher come new interpretations of old power by man's new might. Spirit is man's new power if he is to be truly mighty in his civilization. Only Art and Religion can bring this new vision as reality to a nation. Only the free man brings freedom. This new sense of life comes to his own nation and to the modern world as well. So Art and Architecture, soon his Religion too, must be new. The spiritual dignity of this new humane life for mankind, is the Spirit of Man himself sacrosanct. America has made this commitment. How are we to live up to the promise of that commitment? Where find the true sacrifices by and for this new man in this new world we call the United States of America?

This new release of the spirit of man comes to pass in our own good turn of time. Therefore to architecture comes a new sense of scale; the scale of the human being, man himself. Greater freedom all along the line of habitation becomes not only his desire but his privilege. A great simplicity is now his; the simplicity of perfect organism may be his in what he does. Human dignity based upon union of man's physical nature with his spiritual sensibilities.

His philosophy henceforward will cherish this freedom he has accepted and is endeavoring to establish for himself. But he has not yet wrought this new philosophy into terms of his modern life as the old philosophy of the ancient primitives was wrought into theirs. When he has done this, his dangerous new tools instead of the practiced human hand will be used by him to make his liberation not only wishful theory but actual life — incomparable. But if they are not so used by him, a greater enslavement than ever now looms for him. Man either learns to use for humanity his new facilities or he perishes by them. A true sense of this new power in building-construction is basic to his civilization now. In architecture he will still find the basis of his new culture. At last this realization is dawning upon him.

In the realm of his own imagination come forms found only in freedom of spirit. Space outflowing instead of static containment. Liberation a fulfillment. Architecture no longer any kind of fortification but generously spacious and plastic. Thus expression of the new freedom no longer aggrandizes exterior forms of power but truly liberates man's sense of himself as Man. Instead of fortifying life by extraneous means and remaining subservient to ancient earthly gods — now comes our revelation that man conceives nothing higher than the soul of man himself and when he interprets himself from within, his outward expression will be all the heaven he could imagine and so desire. We call him thus, in himself, great Architecture. Trusting the great "becoming" as always he is in himself the omnipotent Idea. Forever becoming, always on his way to life eternal.

Thus comes to us the new sense of the true building: free in design, poetic but no less, even more, invulnerable shelter from the elements. Space free — space *flowing outward* by way of forms appropriate to life and circumstance. Appropriate *in human scale,* significance comes alive and works for mankind more at one with the character of man's spiritual nature.

For instance, here see the third dimension becoming a fourth; the architect's sensibilities throughout as creative artist becoming aware of democracy in a medium appropriate to his new life. Daily needs are no longer met by the old inappropriate architecture. Sound and practical these poetic liberations are when seen. The straight-line, stream-lined, flat-plane effects appropriate to proper use of his new advantages in this age of the machine are quiet but in the quick. Architecture is of elemental beauty again and of increased service to mankind.

## THE EUROPEAN CONTRADICTION

This concept of architecture as organic, as expression from within outward, is twentieth century — a new sense of building entirely. The concept a "natural." Out of this concept comes interpretation of the third as a fourth dimension: the third seen not as thickness but as depth. Independent of any European influences whatsoever this twentieth century contribution, as a negation of previous concepts of architecture went to Germany, 1910 or earlier. And this — although originally an *affirmative* negation — became, in the European nineteenth century contribution, a negative affirmation, still applying to the old bridge engineer's concept of steel framing — structure from the outside in — the brittle box emphasized as brittle. Unless much mistaken in what I see at the core of the effort I am afraid it has too long remained so. Now past the middle of the twentieth century, European architecture is still nineteenth century in concept. Louis Sullivan's buildings were nineteenth century prophetic; the European contribution is nineteenth century reminiscent.

Yet almost all of our architecture here in America still speaks with foreign accent. First the accent was British, then the accent was French, then German.

Simple truths of the nature of the originating idea of modern architecture from the outside in and the space concept — are just beginning to be recognized by our critics. The new architecture was never so much "functional" as it was dynamic humanism. Solidly based upon the new humanities and modern sciences as the cornerstone of our genuine American culture, it has lacked penetrating criticism. Dynamic forms true to democratic sentiment would become more expanded and extended had such interpretation been forthcoming: life would have become by now more humane, imaginative and colorful. All this has passed unrecognized by current "criticism." In the practice of the dated cliché, our modern riches have gone by default into a sterile classicism: the steel framing of the box. (Don't go near the window!) The crack in the picture-window is widening.

## DISCOVERY

From the prophetic nineteenth century work of Louis H. Sullivan, twentieth century architecture issued by way of the Hillside Home School, the Larkin Building, Unity Temple, the Coonley and Robie houses, the Imperial Hotel and the block houses (The Millard, etc.) of 1921 on.

In this connection, I remember Kuno Francke, German exchange-professor of aesthetics at Harvard (one of Theodore Roosevelt's exchange-professors), came from Harvard to Oak Park (1909) with his charming wife. Herr Professor came to see the work I had done of which he had heard at Harvard. Astonished and pleased by what he saw already accomplished when he came: the Coonley, Robie, Winslow and Cheney houses; Unity Temple; designs for other buildings; he urged me to come to Germany. Said Kuno Francke, "My people are groping, only superficially, for what I see you doing organically: your people are not ready for you. Your life here will be wasted. But my people are ready for you. They will reward you. Fifty years, at least, will pass before your people will be ready for you."

I did not want to go to Germany. I could not speak German. Fascinated by what I was already doing, I declined this invitation. Professor Francke soon returned to Germany. Several months later came the proposition from Wasmuth (well-known publisher in Berlin of art works) proposing to publish the work Kuno Francke had seen (all of it) if I would come to Germany to supervise preparation. A few months later, cancelling obligations of every nature in the field of architecture and at home, I went; risking the worm's-eye view of society I felt must follow. There in Germany and Italy I lived and worked for a year. In the little Villino Belvedere of Fiesole, massive door of the villino opening directly upon the steep, narrow little Via Verdi of the ancient old Roman town on the hill above Florence — I found sanctuary. Just below the little villino spread downward to ancient Firenze the slope where so many distinguished refugees from foreign lands had found sanctuary and were still finding harbor. Most of that year — 1910 — I worked preparing the forthcoming publication in German, *Ausgefuehrte Bauten und Entwuerfe*. Accordingly published in Berlin 1910-11. German edition promptly absorbed. Unfortunately the part of the edition bought for American distribution by two of my good clients, Francis W. Little and Darwin D. Martin, was temporarily stored below ground-level at Taliesin, previous to arrangements for distribution. The entire portion of the edition meant for America was consumed in the fire destroying the first Taliesin — 1912. (First of three destructive fires at Taliesin.) Smoke rose from the smouldering mass below grade for several days. So America saw little of this original publication in German unless imported. But one whole copy only and about one-half of another now stays at Taliesin with me. The entire work was more cheaply reprinted (smaller in size) in Germany later — also reprinted, in still smaller format, by Japan. *Cahiers d'Art*, France, published a resume in 1911. These publications have all but disappeared.

## INCIDENTAL

Unfortunately, most of the original drawings made for this publication I took with me to Japan when commissioned to build the Emperor's "Teikoku Hotel" in Tokyo. Disappeared — perhaps because the Japanese covet, and cherish, the work of their masters; therefore of other masters.

For instance, a famous Japanese poet himself wrote a sign "Please keep off the grass"; set it up on the freshly seeded lawn in front of his new house. Every morning the sign was gone. But he kept on for several more days, posting a new sign each morning which he had himself written. Each morning the sign was gone. In despair the poet asked advice of a friend: Said the friend, "Employ a sign-writer to make the sign." The poet did. The sign stayed.

## ORNAMENT

Plasticity, a *quality* new to architecture, is directly related to elasticity. What plasticity is to architecture, as I have been using that term, may need explanation. Somehow, as a boy of fourteen — probably deduced from my memory of Victor Hugo's prophecy, read in *Notre Dame* — I had come to regard the pilaster with aversion because it was applied to the face of a wall as pretended construction. So the pilaster became a symbol of falsity to me, or mere applied decoration. By then I was seeing the buildings of European Renaissance themselves as a kind of *pilaster*, as later I learned to see the Greek entablature and cornice as carpenter-work in stone. The Parthenon was really a copy in stone of an Etruscan wooden temple. So soon I throw all that in with pilaster! Both were the kind of arty-pretense I had already learned to call "constructed decoration" — that is to say, ornament found out of place in violation of the organic nature of materials and construction. Ornament if organic was never *on* the thing but *of* it; therefore little of the ornamentation of the Greek orders seemed more than merely pictorial. Charming but appliqué. This thought had appeared and remained with me: any true plasticity would be a quality *of* the thing itself, never be on it (applied to it). This meant positive negation of most classic ornament of the many "classic" styles. Plasticity therefore dictated ornament as one with structural or interior quality; its place was intrinsic. Yes. In architecture ornament should be organic in character: See nature! Building constructions embodying these ideals were built by myself Midwest, 1893, and seen in Germany by the Wasmuth publication just mentioned. At least as early as 1910, these were explained by myself as organic plasticity; the term I first applied to more humble buildings — dwellings. But "plastic" might apply with truth to all ornament in construction. Architecture by nature was susceptible to ornament. If old forms were denied, new ones should be capable of great affirmation. Humanity in the great mother-art would be seen in buildings for America's new place in time. Architecture might, but not by way of plasticity alone, become new and fit for a culture natural to us.

## INTEGRATION INTRINSIC

When these new integers are able to cultivate and enrich the technical uses of art in organic architecture, new significance will have come to the citizen. The vital changes in his life could be interpreted to him and affirmed by his modern art. Were architects to become more interested in Architecture than in architects, architecture might not only tell posterity how man was in our time but *present* him for what he aimed to be. In the spiritual fibre of new ideas, his architecture yet does not tell! To be thus richer in culture he must be alive, more wide awake than man ever was before. This should be because he is better equipped, commands extraordinary facilities now. His responsibility widens with his own stature. All is now fresh opportunity for him; if still beyond his reach — as his lack of vision now would seem to indicate — in his humanity a quality "always sings" and is the virtuous life ever so "beautiful as the morning"?

The young American has yet to learn that freedom is earned "from within": a persistent vision that never for long leaves the man who is in love with the sense of democratic life. Freedom is promised to him by the nature of his government. But government, the policeman, can only guard not bestow freedom. Culture and government dislike each other by nature. In architecture, eventually, ideal freedom is up to the individual.

Exuberant and serene as this new architecture is it should no longer shy at the term "romantic" because organic free-thinking and building *are* by nature romantic; rich in romance of the human heart as ever. "Romantic?" Yes. This romance already stirs in young America because in the young the essence of character is always the originating idea of form. Character is no less fate in architecture today than ever in the life of the man of past ages.

Wherever they are found, organic buildings will belong, solidly based upon the *human* nature of elemental Nature. This nature-wise philosophy of architecture can never resort to the expedient cliché. The petty bias of personal taste can no longer hide either excrescence or spiritual poverty in the name of style. As natural building proceeds, the individual will see building as he is learning to see life. Idea to idea, idea to form and form to function, buildings designed to liberate and expand, not contain and confine, the richer, deeper elements of nature.

## THE IDEA

The idea? In philosophy, the idea is ancient as Laotze but — in building for the occupation of modern man — as modern as the future. Poetic is prophetic insight. The genius of highly cultivated emigrés first gave birth to our nation. Now must come those who make the nation a worthy reality! Such truth of being will characterize those who will eventually bear this fruit, however long neglected — or worse, distorted — either by success or by fear.

So "classic" now is far worse for the cause of freedom than ever classic was before because fresh light has now dawned from fruitful sources within upon man's imperishable soul. If it is neglected, we lose our American birthright.

The social influences of all that science can do, if not interpreted by the creative artist, may be more sterilizing than fructifying. Intellectual is not necessarily intelligent either. At the Chicago World's Fair, American architecture sadly learned that popular sentimentality has nothing in common with true sentiment and unless, in the architecture of today, the new tools of this era of the machine come in for interpretation and human use in artists' hands a heavy liability will result.

## STANDARDIZED

Man in his upended street must know he is becoming a mere numerical item of convenience; on the way to being a thing. His inherent instinct for love and beauty is not only becoming suspect but, in spite of all intent, useless to society. He sees the human creature atrophy as he sees poverty of imagination in much "modern art," so-called. But it was Walt Whitman himself who raised the perpendicular hand to declare: "It is provided in the essence of things that from any fruition of success no matter what, shall come forth something to make a greater struggle necessary." This is what is now coming forth in our architecture as in our life.

SIDE VIEW

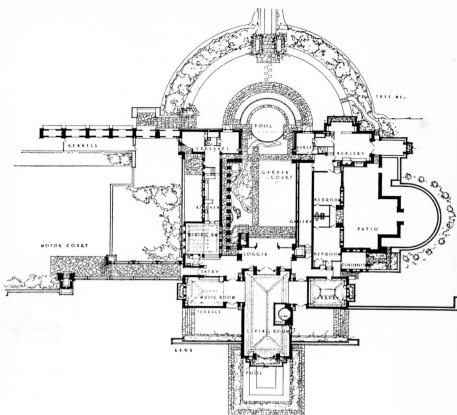

1917-20. BARNSDALL ("HOLLYHOCK") HOUSE, OLIVE HILL, LOS ANGELES, CALIFORNIA. "THE FIRST OF THE CALIFORNIA DWELLINGS AND A CHARACTERISTIC CALIFORNIA ROMANZA, EMBODYING THE CHARACTERISTIC FEATURES OF THE REGION FOR A CLIENT WHO LOVED THEM AND THE THEATER. SHE NAMED THE HOUSE HOLLYHOCK HOUSE AND ASKED THAT THE FLOWER BE USED AS A MOTIVE IN THE DECORATION OF THE PLACE. THE WOODEN STRUCTURE OF THE PERIOD AND PLACE PLASTERED WITH CONCRETE AND TRIMMED WITH CAST STONE."

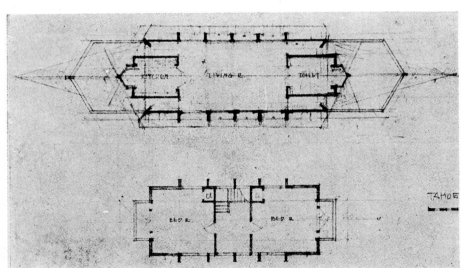

1922.  TAHOE BARGE, FAMILY TYPE

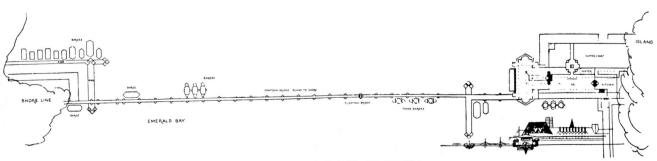

1922.   PROJECT, TAHOE SUMMER COLONY, EMERALD BAY, LAKE TAHOE, CALIFORNIA

TAHOE CABIN, SHORE TYPE

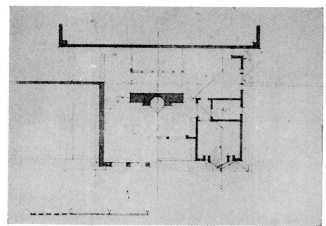

TAHOE CABIN
FIR TREE TYPE

1922.   PROJECT, TAHOE SUMMER COLONY, LAKE TAHOE, CALIFORNIA

TAHOE CABIN, FIR TREE TYPE

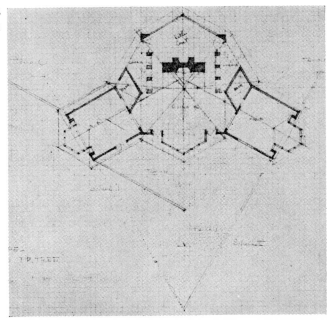

140

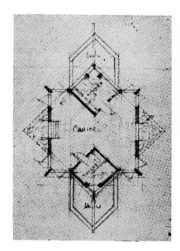

BARGE, "FALLEN LEAF"

BARGE FOR TWO

TAHOE CABIN, WIGWAM TYPE

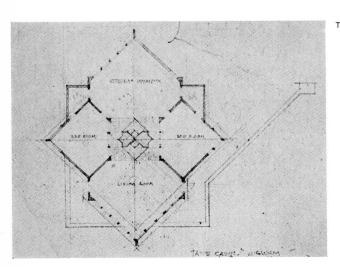

LODGE TYPE

1922. TAHOE SUMMER COLONY, LAKE TAHOE, CALIFORNIA

1921-23. MILLARD HOUSE ("LA MINIATURA"), PASADENA, CALIFORNIA—"THE FIRST CONCRETE BLOCK HOUSE TO EMPLOY THE TEXTILE-BLOCK SYSTEM INVENTED BY MYSELF SEVERAL YEARS BEFORE. A HOLLOW WALL FORMED OF 3-INCH THICK CONCRETE BLOCKS WAS REINFORCED IN THE JOINTS BOTH WAYS; STEEL CROSS TIES PLACED EVERY THIRD COURSE; JOINTS POURED WITH THIN CEMENT GROUT. AN EARTHQUAKE PROOF LIGHT CONSTRUCTION BUT NO PERMIT COULD BE ISSUED BECAUSE CONCRETE GOT TOO BIG A PREFERENCE."

MILLARD HOUSE

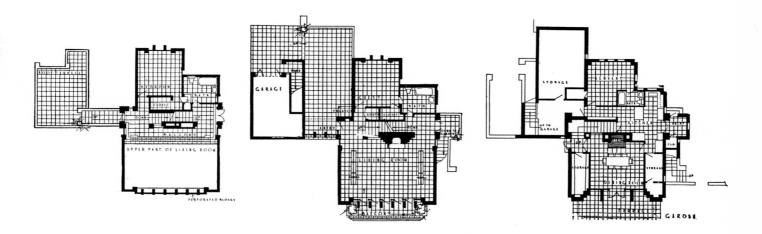

145

1922-23.  STORER HOUSE, LOS ANGELES, CALIFORNIA

STORER HOUSE

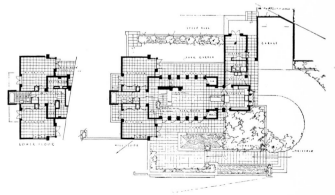

LOWER FLOOR PLAN, LEFT—UPPER FLOOR PLAN, RIGHT

147

1922-24.  ENNIS HOUSE, LOS ANGELES, CALIFORNIA

ENNIS HOUSE

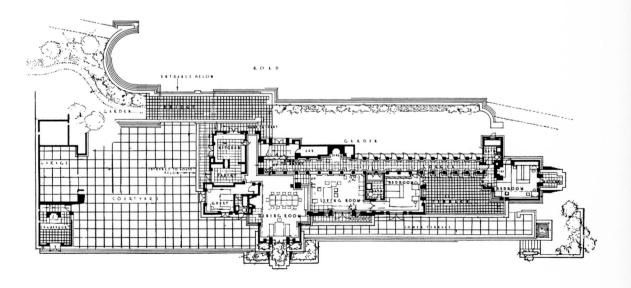

1924.  FREEMAN HOUSE, LOS ANGELES, CALIFORNIA

FREEMAN HOUSE

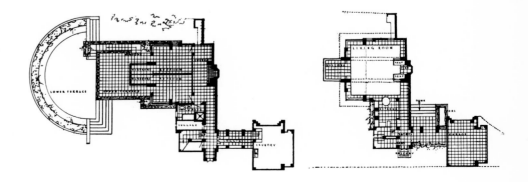

1924. PROJECT, NAKOMA COUNTRY CLUB, MADISON, WISCONSIN.
"GRAVITY HEAT, FIRST USED IN 1915 IN THE IMPERIAL HOTEL IN
TOKYO, WAS PLANNED FOR THE NAKOMA COUNTRY CLUB BUT THAT
INDIANESQUE AFFAIR STAYED IN THE FORM OF A BEAUTIFUL PLAN.
GRAVITY HEAT, ALSO DESIGNED IN 1936 FOR THE JOHNSON ADMIN-
ISTRATION BUILDING, WAS FIRST A FINISHED PRODUCT IN 1937
IN THE JACOBS HOUSE—THE FIRST FLOOR-HEATED HOUSE IN THE
UNITED STATES." (FOR ANOTHER VERSION OF THIS USONIAN HOUSE
TYPE, SEE THE ROSENBAUM HOUSE, 1939 (PAGE 167)

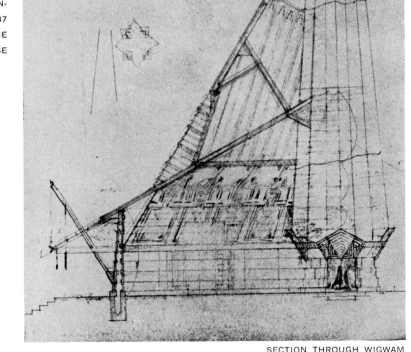

SECTION THROUGH WIGWAM

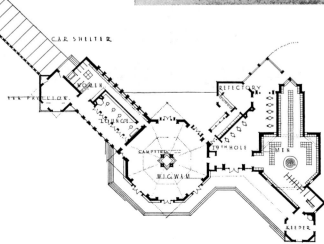

PART THREE

# CONCERNING THE THIRD DIMENSION

**ERROR I**

Today, around the circumference of architectural thought, basic error still exists concerning the new concept I have stated of the good old third dimension — usually seen as thickness, weight, a solid. Sublimated by organic architecture, it is interpreted as *depth*. The "*depth*-dimension" — really a fourth now — the sense of space. Perhaps the fourth as sought by the European cubist? The element we call *space* given a new concept. Listen to Laotze again: "The reality of the building consists not in the walls and roof but in the space within to be lived in." Witness organic architecture.

**ERROR II**

Concerns our universal power-tool, the Machine. The machine is accepted by organic architecture only as a tool to a greater freedom: new power to manipulate new materials by new strategy. But the machine has already been so far misused, taken aside from culture, as to become deadly facility, mostly in the wrong direction. By too many architects it is used as a motif or an excuse for one. Or else they are used by it.

Even now, sixty years later, its true significance is rarely grasped and used for what it really is. Promoted now by too many "moderns" in architecture, it is reduced to the status of a ritual, or at least to an end in itself; exaggerating quantity at expense to the quality of human significance.

The appeal of this mechanical facility appears to be to the "pictorial" in art and architecture — an evasion of the nature of construction: the two-dimensional poverty of design seen in the facades of current steel-framing of the box added to this purely negative cliché. Now, we have too many stale derivatives of the straight-line, flat-plane effects originally contributed by organic architecture to Europeans in the early days when it was the great negation. The effects then were seminal but the depth-language of that early time is badly translated when it is separated from its original concept of the depth-dimension. So misunderstood, this dimension again appears as thickness instead of depth. What made these early effects — wholly new to architecture then — possible some fifty years ago and enables them to continue, seems yet to be obscure. Therefore various phases of this original straight-line, flat-plane architecture are still mistaken for negation as, in a sense, they originally were — especially their grammar as it appeared until about 1908. But then came another beginning, revolutionary in character — amazing the consequences — still revelation: A further concept of plan and form to go on with the cantilever and continuity — suitable to new materials and as genuine machine-age technique — but grown richer in human content. No longer confined to the earlier "affirmative negation" the new effects of affirmation, earlier only implied, were now directly involved; and misunderstood by hatchet-men following "the moderns." Having been attracted by the original negation they remain, more or less (if unconsciously) negative.

Commercialized as these latter-day two-dimensional facades appear: empty mirrors or emaciated steel-framed cages criss-crossed, they seem to have no more vitality as architecture of the depth-dimension than the radiator front of a motor car, a bird-cage, a glass box at the zoo or a goldfish globe. These box facades are topped with a flat invisible lid in order to emphasize this box effect. The steel box-frame buildings of modern architecture now make a church, a house, a factory, or a hotel, all appear much alike — creating an impression somewhat similar to that made by a horse with his ears laid back. So-called "modern" architecture has therefore gone as ambiguous as it has gone "styleward" (soon to call itself the new "classic") instead of toward a richer expression of the liberation of human beings made possible by the new facilities of our time. But, though the early ideas of organic design have been exploited blindly, or wilfully, their fundamentals are actually not much damaged except in point of time-lapse. Again unreasonable delay on the part of education and government.

Notwithstanding any abortion, organic architecture is for our own country still on an upward way to richer expressions of our freedom and superior technology, growing out of love of human nature. I still believe that architects are all that is the matter with architecture. I have therefore not yet joined the A.I.A. Instead of the American Institute of *Architects,* as I have said, they should make the letters A.I.A. stand for the American Institute of *Architecture* — and mean just that.

## ORGANIC ORNAMENT

"Such as the life is, so is the form." Can the Ethiopian change his skin or the leopard change his spots? Or the turtle be without the pattern of his shell? Expression of the constitution of nature is emphasized, unified, clarified, *identified* by what we call Ornament? True architectural form has innate significance of character expressed and enhanced by the creative architect's organic uses of organic ornament. As melody is in music ornament is in architecture *revelation* of the poetic-principle, with character and significance. Ornament is as natural to architecture of the genus Man as the turtle's shell is to the genus Turtle. Inevitable as plumage to the bird: natural as the form of any seashell; appropriate as scales of the fish or leaves of the tree or the blossom of a blooming plant.

So every living thing bears innate witness to the need for love, expressing the poetic principle by what we call "pattern": visible in all organism. Creation as eye-music is no less expressive than ear-music because it too is heart-music, appealing too, to human life at the very core. Both melody and ornament reach us by way of the soul of all Creation and as we are made we respond.

By human faculties man is able to produce natural melody of a permanent kind to give more pregnant significance to his habitation. Humanly speaking ornament is true attribute of all human culture. To say, ornament is genuine —

is to say it is indigenous. Ornament is intrinsic to the being human of the human being.


No! is always easier to say than Yes. In this matter of integrity of architecture a sense of honor in the human individual has its counterpart. Sympathy and kindness, fine sentiment in the realm of the human heart are in human conduct as the grace and beauty of ornament are to organic architecture. This beautiful quality of thought in the organic constitution of building-construction is fundamentally affirmative. Never can it be negative except as a preliminary preparation for some such affirmation.


## ROMANCE

The eternal Law of Change proceeds. Development has wrought and multiplies as growth among us — or subtracts the past. We are increased or diminished — perhaps destroyed. Evasion, imposition, supposition, suppression, distortion, foolish misinformation all notwithstanding, change proceeds, inexorable, and nature her custom holds. The philosophic center-line of future action in the realm of art is thus daily becoming more evident as the changing current of humane thought in human beings. This old-fashioned term "romantic," too, so long and still so often meaning mere affectation or sentimentality is become liberated and liberating. Architecture is truly romantic. There should lie in the very science and poetry of structure the inspired love of Nature. This is what we should and we do now call Romantic.

The ceaseless overtones and intones of space, when developed as the new reality in architecture, go on, tone upon tone, as they do in the music of Beethoven or Bach, Vivaldi or Palestrina. Like music-totality every good building has this poise, floats, at home on its site as a swan on its lake. Much of the "modern," devoid of this innate sense of music, makes factories of our studios, churches and schools. Education, our greatest busyness, is our greatest deficiency in this matter because it lacks courage as well as enlightenment. It still calls ornament a form of embellishment and, regardless of its poetry, regards it as an impractical luxury. Wherever the question of an *indigenous* American culture comes up to be either appraised or acted upon, the question of its expediency arises, and the expedient is the "pay-off" in terms of money. The cart thus inevitably put before the horse.

But if you listen! You will sometimes hear the language of the poetic principle spoken. And nevertheless, an infinite variety of indigenous art-expressions still come and go in spite of us, especially in architecture. To me, the principles of affirmation were alive and operative even within the original negation, say that of the Larkin Building in Buffalo, New York, as early as 1904, or, about the same time, Unity Temple, Oak Park, or the Hillside Home School I built for my aunts, 1902. These buildings show the principles and should by this time have "come into school." "From inside out" had there been firmly established as a better basis for any criticism directed against, or for, the life of such architecture as lived in our midst.

This is largely the fault of such criticism as reaches us in so many mediums: none of them deep enough or wide enough to see architecture as the cornerstone of our culture, no less than it has been the cornerstone of culture from time immemorial.


## THE CRITIC

How is he made? Oftentimes bitter, sometimes sweet, seldom even wide-awake, architectural criticism of "the modern" wholly lacks inspiration or any qualification because it lacks the appreciation that is love: the flame essential to profound understanding. Only as criticism is the fruit of such experience will it ever be able truly to appraise anything. Else the spirit of true criteria is lacking. That spirit is love and love alone can understand. So art criticism is usually sour and superficial today because it would seem to know all about everything but understand nothing. Usually the public prints afford no more than a kind of irresponsible journalese wholly dependent upon some form of comparison, commercialization or pseudo-personal opinion made public. Critics may have minds of their own, but what chance have they to use them when experience in creating the art they write about is rarely theirs? So whatever they may happen to learn, and you learn from them, is very likely put over *on* both of you as it was put over on them. Truth is seldom *in* the critic; and either good or bad, what comes from him is seldom his. Current criticism is something to take always on suspicion, if taken at all.

## USONIA

Samuel Butler, author of *The Way of All Flesh,* originator of the modern realistic novel, in his *Erewhon* ("nowhere" spelled backwards) pitied us for having no name of our own. "The United States" did not appear to him a good title for us as a nation and the word "American" belonged to us only in common with a dozen or more countries. So he suggested USONIAN — roots of the word in the word unity or in *union.* This to me seemed appropriate. So I have often used this word when needing reference to our own country or style.

Imagine for a moment what fertile Usonian manifestations of well-disciplined human imagination our environment might be today if, instead of the panders to European dead-ends, creative thought and feeling had been encouraged, the creative sense of space in architecture properly recognized — and now become intrinsic! If teachers had become *enriched by such experience,* and cultivated it as basic element of their own education, they would have been free to cultivate our democratic vision, might have buttressed our American spirit against the confusion and conformity that beset us now. With their help we might now be able to see spiritual entity as beauty — beauty as ethical — and ethics as more important than morals, or money, or laws. If the meaning of the word Usonian had only thus become truly characteristic of the unity of our national life we would have earned this title, and Usonia would be ours.

## SCIENCE AND THE SCIENTIST

The scientist: he who takes life apart but is unable to put it back together again to live. Scientists practice invention, addition and subtraction — but in the teaching of architecture they should not continue to be mistaken as creative

1925.   PROJECT, GLADNEY HOUSE, FORT WORTH, TEXAS

ARCHITECT'S STUDY, TALIESIN

1925. TALIESIN III. SPRING GREEN, WISCONSIN. "TALIESIN NORTH (HOME OF THE TALIESIN FELLOWSHIP) WAS FIRST BUILT IN 1911. TWICE DESTROYED BY FIRE IT HAS RISEN FOR THE THIRD TIME FROM ITS ASHES AND IS TODAY APPROACHING THE COMPLETENESS AND QUALITY ORIGINALLY HOPED FOR BY ITS ARCHITECT. IT IS A HOUSE OF THE NORTH AND PECULIAR TO THE LOW ROLLING HILLS OF THE REGION—SOUTHERN WISCONSIN. THE TERRACES COMMAND VIEWS OF THE VALLEY BELOW AND THE WISCONSIN RIVER BEYOND. TALIESIN IS A WELSH WORD MEANING 'SHINING BROW.' THE PLACE IS BUILT AROUND THE BROW OF THE HILL—NOT ON THE HILL."

1928. STUDY, SCHOOLHOUSE FOR NEGRO CHILDREN, ROSENWALD FOUNDATION, LA JOLLA, CALIFORNIA

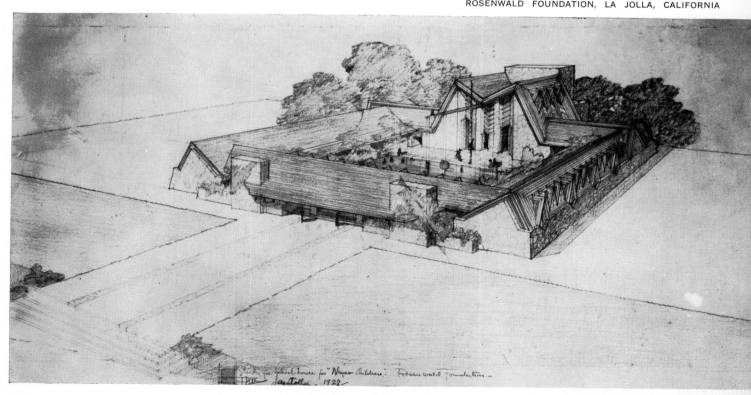

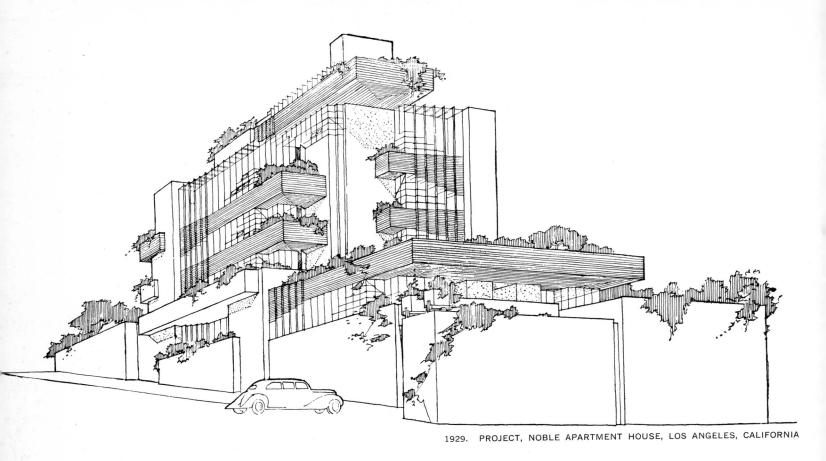

1929.   PROJECT, NOBLE APARTMENT HOUSE, LOS ANGELES, CALIFORNIA

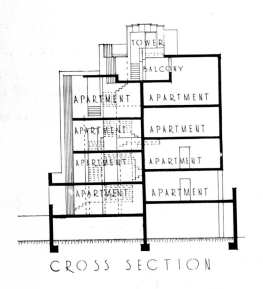

CROSS SECTION

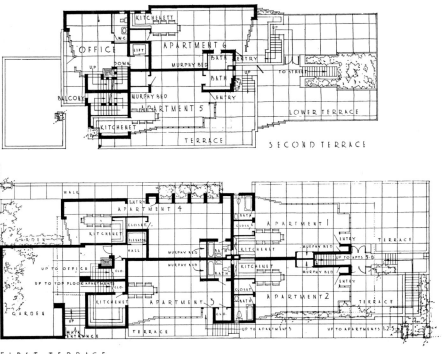

SECOND TERRACE

FIRST TERRACE

1936. KAUFMANN HOUSE, "FALLINGWATER," BEAR RUN, PENNSYLVANIA. "IN A BEAUTIFUL FOREST, A SOLID HIGH ROCK-LEDGE RISING BESIDE A WATERFALL . . . THE NATURAL THING SEEMED TO BE TO CANTILEVER THE HOUSE FROM THAT ROCK-BANK OVER THE FALLING WATER. THE FIRST HOUSE IN MY EXPERIENCE TO BE BUILT OF REINFORCED CONCRETE — SO THE FORM TOOK THE GRAMMAR OF THAT TYPE OF CONSTRUCTION." (SECTION, BELOW)

1938. TALIESIN WEST, PARADISE VALLEY, NEAR PHOENIX, ARIZONA, "WAS STARTED BY THE TALIESIN FELLOWSHIP AND HAS BEEN AN OBJECT LESSON IN CONSTRUCTION EVER SINCE TO THE APPRENTICES WHO CAME TO LIVE AND WORK THERE WITH THE ARCHITECT. THE COMPLETE CHANGE IN TERRAIN CAUSED A COMPLETE CHANGE IN FORM. A NEW TECHNIQUE WAS NECESSARY AND WHILE IT IS DIFFICULT TO IMAGINE A GREATER VARIETY OF ARCHITECTURAL CONTRAST THAN SEEMS TO EXIST BETWEEN TALIESIN NORTH AND TALIESIN WEST THE SAME PRINCIPLES ARE AT WORK AND THERE IS BASIC SYMPATHY BETWEEN THE TWO STRUCTURES." THIS VIEW IS FROM THE TERRACE BESIDE THE DRAUGHTING ROOM TOWARD DINING ROOM AND POOL AT RIGHT.

VIEW FROM LIVING ROOM THROUGH GARDEN COURT. "TALIESIN WEST IS A HEAVY MASONRY MASSED CONSTRUCTION TOPPED WITH REDWOOD TIMBERING CARRYING FRAMES UPON WHICH CANVAS HAS BEEN STRETCHED TO MAKE A TEXTILE OVERHEAD. THE PLEASANTEST LIGHTING IMAGINABLE IS THE RESULT. THE INSPIRATION FOR TALIESIN WEST CAME FROM THE SAME SOURCE AS THE EARLY AMERICAN PRIMITIVES AND THERE ARE CERTAIN RESEMBLANCES, BUT NOT INFLUENCES."

1939.  ROSENBAUM HOUSE, FLORENCE, ALABAMA, STREET FRONT

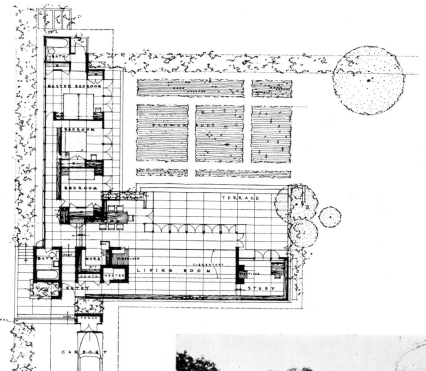

THE USONIAN HOUSE TYPE. "A MODEST HOUSE THIS USONIAN HOUSE, A DWELLING PLACE THAT HAS NO FEELING AT ALL FOR THE 'GRAND' EXCEPT AS THE HOUSE EXTENDS ITSELF IN THE FLAT PARALLEL TO THE GROUND . . . A COMPANION TO THE HORIZON . . . LOVING THE GROUND WITH THE NEW SENSE OF SPACE, LIGHT AND FREEDOM—TO WHICH OUR U. S. A. IS ENTITLED."

VIEW FROM GARDEN

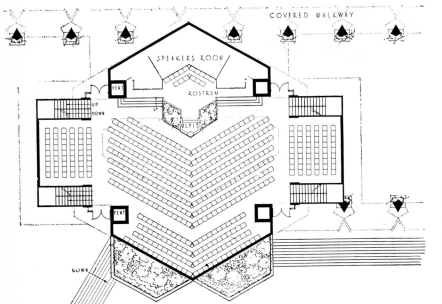

COVERED WALKWAY

SPEAKERS ROOM

ROSTRUM

VENT

UP
DOWN

UP

PULPIT

VENT

DOWN

1940. ANN PFEIFFER CHAPEL, FLORIDA SOUTHERN COLLEGE, LAKELAND, FLORIDA. "THIS PROJECT FOR DR. LUDD M. SPIVEY IS STILL GROWING, PROBABLY THE ONE ENTIRELY MODERN CAMPUS AMONG OUR EDUCATIONAL INSTITUTIONS. THE OVER-ALL PLAN IS FLORIDIAN IN CHARACTER CONSISTING OF DEEPLY SHADED WINDING ESPLANADES BETWEEN BUILDINGS OFTEN EVENTUATING INTO BUILDINGS. THE WHOLE IS FLORIDA—SOUTHERN AND PLASTIC IN FEELING, RICHLY PLANTED." (SEE PAGES 234, 235)

1943. SOLOMON R. GUGGENHEIM MUSEUM, NEW YORK CITY, PRELIMINARY VERSION

"WE ARE NOT BUILDING A CELLULAR COMPOSITION OF COMPARTMENTS, BUT ONE WHERE ALL IS ONE GREAT SPACE ON A CONTINUOUS FLOOR . . . THE WHOLE IS CAST IN CONCRETE MORE AN EGGSHELL IN FORM THAN A CRISSCROSS STICK STRUCTURE. THE CONCRETE IS RENDERED STRONG ENOUGH EVERYWHERE TO DO ITS WORK BY FILAMENTS OF STEEL, SEPARATE OR IN MESH. STRUCTURAL CALCULATIONS ARE THUS THOSE OF CANTILEVER AND CONTINUITY RATHER THAN THE CONVENTIONAL POST AND BEAM FORMULA. THE NET RESULT OF SUCH CONSTRUCTION IS GREATER REPOSE, AN ATMOSPHERE OF THE UNBROKEN WAVE—NO MEETING OF THE EYE WITH ANGULAR OR ABRUPT CHANGES OF FORM. ALL IS AS ONE AND AS NEAR INDESTRUCTIBLE AS IT IS POSSIBLE TO MAKE A BUILDING."

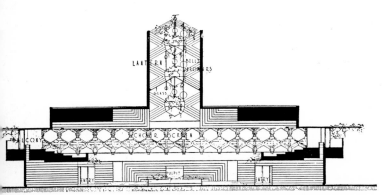

ION, ANN PFEIFFER CHAPEL, FLORIDA SOUTHERN COLLEGE

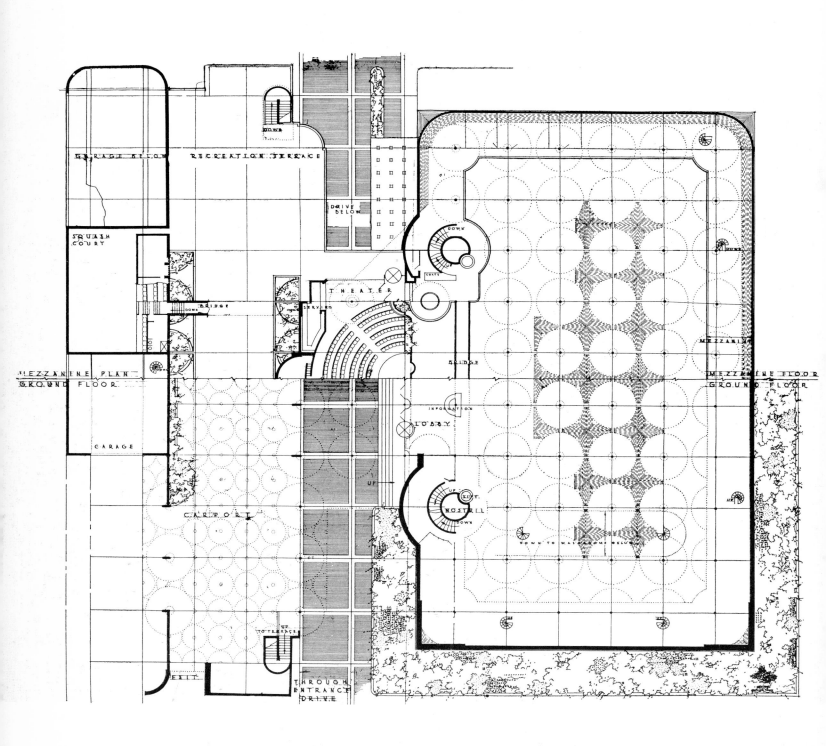

GLASS TUBING LAID UP LIKE BRICKS IN A WALL COMPOSE ALL THE LIGHTING SURFACES. LIGHT ENTERS THE BUILDING WHERE THE
[COR]NICE USED TO BE. IN THE INTERIOR THE BOXLIKE STRUCTURE VANISHED COMPLETELY. THE WALLS CARRYING THE GLASS RIBBING
[AR]E OF HARD RED BRICK AND RED KASOTA SANDSTONE. THE ENTIRE FABRIC IS REINFORCED CONCRETE, COLD-DRAWN MESH USED
[FO]R REINFORCEMENT."

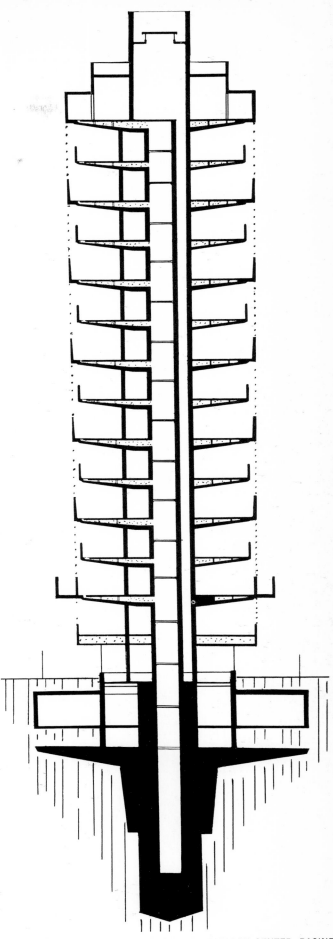

1947.   TOWER, S. C. JOHNSON AND SON RESEARCH CENTER, RACINE, WISCONSIN—"UP IN THE AIR AROUND A GIANT CENTRAL STACK WITH FLOORS BRANCHING FROM IT, HAVING CLEAR LIGHT AND SPACE ALL AROUND EACH FLOOR."

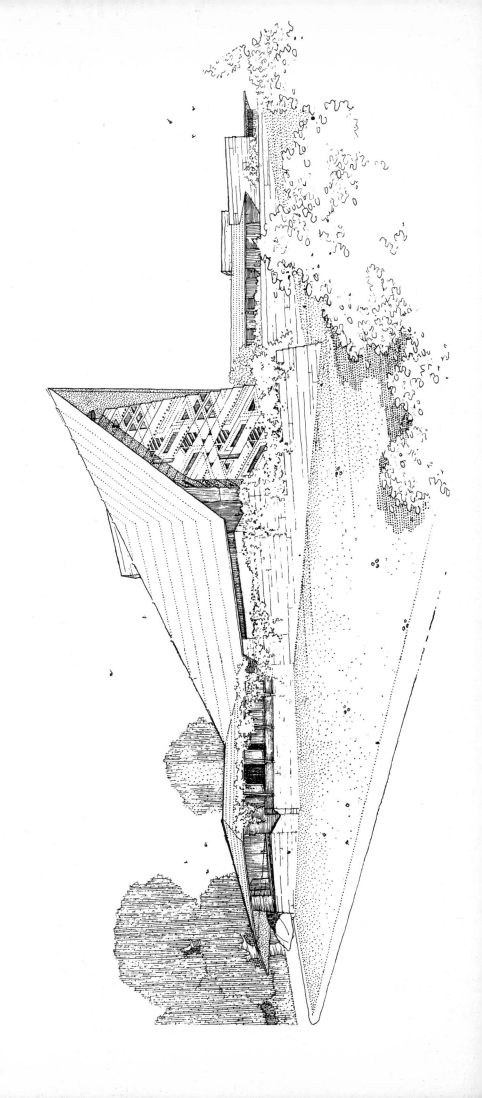

1949. FIRST UNITARIAN CHURCH, MADISON, WISCONSIN—"ORIGINALLY IN-TENDED BY THIS UNITARIAN SOCIETY TO BE BUILT DOWNTOWN. DECENTRALIZA-TION IN MIND, THEY WERE PERSUADED TO GO OUT INTO ADJOINING COUNTRY TO BUILD A CHARACTERISTIC SOCIAL CENTER. THE EDIFICE IS BASED UPON THE TRIANGLE (THE SYMBOL OF ASPIRATION) IN THE FORM OF PRAYER AND SYMBOLIZES UNITY ABOVE ALL. THE SINGULARLY TRUSSED ROOF IS COVERED WITH COPPER. WALLS ARE OF NATIVE LIMESTONE."

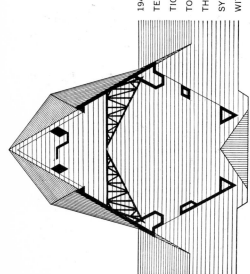

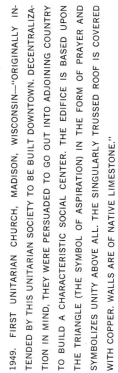

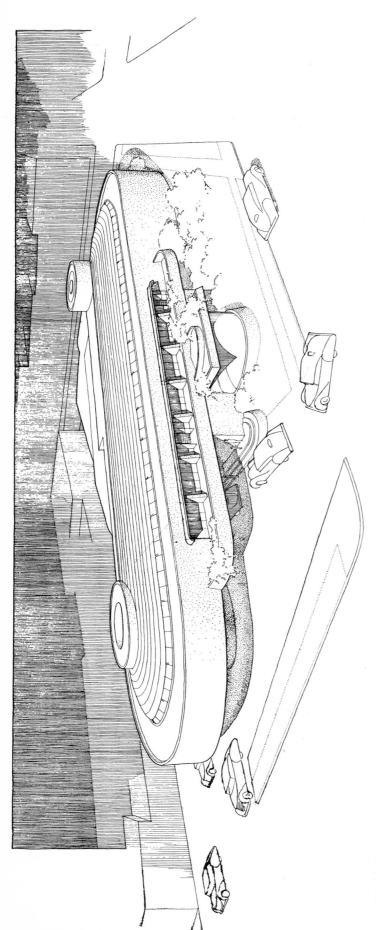

1948. PROJECT, ADELMAN LAUNDRY, MILWAUKEE, WISCONSIN. "THIS 'DRIVE-IN' WAS AN ATTEMPT TO PUT A NOVEL IDEA IN THE LAUNDRY BUSINESS INTO THE PERFECT SHAPE, IDEAL FOR ITS PURPOSE . . . STEEL REINFORCED CONCRETE SLAB CONSTRUCTION. THE BUILDING HAS BEEN PLANNED AS A GREAT OPEN CENTER, WITH A PLENUM-CHAMBER OVERHEAD, FILLED WITH WARM AIR IN WINTER, COOL AIR IN SUMMER, THE AIR DRAWN INTO THE WORKROOMS THEMSELVES BY THE SUCTION OF THE BASEMENT EXHAUST TO WHICH THE BOILER ROOM IS CONNECTED. DINING ROOM AND SERVICE ACCOMMODATIONS ARE IN THE MEZZANINE ABOVE THE PRIVATE OFFICES."

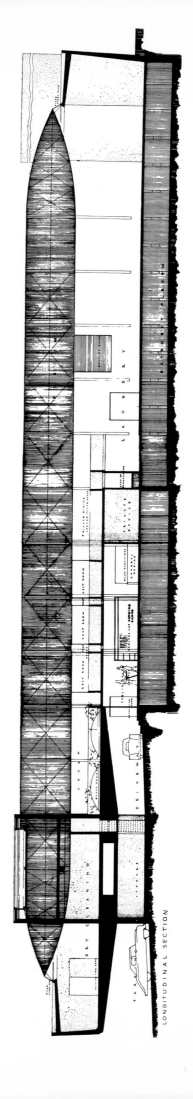

LONGITUDINAL SECTION

themselves. They are one reason why the huge business of education is not on speaking terms with culture and such culture as we now have is not on speaking terms with reality. So long as the scientific, pictorial or business interest comes first in order to make a living, culture — divorced from life as it is lived — will be helpless or false.

## THE SUBSTITUTE

The substitute for art and religion has been science.

Indigenous poetry has been leeched from our common life by the "practical" materialistic ideals of industry, education and government. War — ultimate substitute provided by science. Yet the poet is not yet dead and, as a consequence, we are not.

Would you worship life amid this confusion of today, remember again the prophecy by the ideal Man, "The Kingdom of God is within *you*." By Nature-worship, by way of revelation of your own nature alone, can your God be reached. By this fresh sentiment of individuality that gave America freedom, organic building has come along. If its principles had been comprehended by the hordes of those impressed by its appearance; if its imitators, so quickly attracted by its aspects, had grasped its intrinsic virtue, we would now be well ahead of any controversy now confusing the issue. We might not be called "the only great nation to have proceeded directly from barbarism to degeneracy with no culture of our own in between." The truth is: we are a great experiment still: and all the same a great civilization. But the truth is also we are an amazing tentative culture, in possession of more than we have digested or are able yet to understand. So far as a culture of our *own* is concerned we still thrive on substitutes provided by science in spite of the fact that we *do* now have something to export besides dollars.

It is all too easy for derivatives of culture to thrive in our midst at expense to the original. Society always a coward afraid to acknowledge any debt to origins. How can any substitute ever be good in our nation for the creative artist? Our culture depends on him.

# THE MONUMENTAL

The monumental should now be not so monumental as memorial. Owing to our sovereignty it is high time the scale of the human figure and its elemental, natural rhythms be put into the culture of our architects and by way of characteristic machine-age technique by T-square and triangle made to take the place of the unsightly grandomania of our early days as a nation. Witness our national capital and its progeny, our tributes to greatness. Ironical that a nation devoted to the upholding of law should have become so devoted to illegitimate architecture. But "the monument" is still seen in the mere bigness or tallness that is not in itself natural but tries to match the chronic old syndrome of column, pilaster and cornice. Whereas the modern should have something more noble and appropriate to say. Architecture has no need for monumentality unless as a natural beauty. On any other terms, either public or private, size or tallness is not the point at issue. The question is, has it the significance of beauty natural to *now*.

The wall standing stark is essential monumentality but empty. Such architectural features and proportions as are designed to put the inferiority complex to the soul of man are no longer valid or vital. It was picturesque in the days of empire, kingship and great temporal authority; and may be thrilling and picturesque again when serving a purpose well and we inherit from nature its grandeur. But, such pictorialization as we see in reckless posterism, this sterile negation of the individual, these fixations of his fate rattling the bones of construction in box-like frames, the strident steel criss-cross of these boxes trying to look tall when they can only look big — are all eventually unsatisfactory to the spirit of man. In the nature of life, tall should mean not merely high, but a beautiful expression of aspiration. The soul of modern man has more depth than such architectural masquerade, expression of mere quantity, would indicate. Desire for more imaginative humane expression with deeper feeling still grows outside as well as in our cities due to the sense of the individual's sovereignty in his America. The essential suppression of his spiritual faith will be his curse, if freedom ceases to be beautiful as expression of the American spirit.

In any sincere practice of this fundamental philosophy of building we will find the great means to put the best of man, *living as himself*, into what he builds to live in, live up to and be judged by. If better architects could thus find themselves they would eventually be found by their people. They might see themselves ennobled and built into the hearts of their people by their knowledge of the straight way to serve life as it can be lived today.

## SELF-POSSESSION

Americans need the serenity of spiritual strength in what they build even more than in what they do. Tranquility and repose as a people would be great reward and assurance — always an indispensable quality of freedom. Modern mechanical skills are cheap enough though technical skill is cheated, because it is expected to be only mechanical, not inspired. Architects are wasting skills both ways and so their clients are cheated of what they really have a right to expect: integrity of spirit. Integrity? I believe I see it awakening here and there as a new American civic conscience. The great mother-art of architecture will not fail to envision and ennoble the American life of our future. True to this emancipation the common man standing there beyond will be bravest and best of us and where he belongs.

We — the people — must retrieve this environment of ours already so heavily mortgaged. Both the life of town and country now waste each other. Accelerated by the exaggerated motor car, these interchanges and mortgages are forged by the rail men, the pole-and-wire men, advertising men; the realtor, the so-called "developer" — all defacing life. Call these *conservative?* Conservative should mean faithful maintenance at all costs of the free ideals for the sake of which our forefathers gave to every man in the country a stake in himself, as most glorious of all his privileges. Men truly "conservative" would not tolerate overwhelming violations of life, moving us toward the danger of mediocrity in high places. We should be less likely to allow an expedient conformity to frustrate our growth. Nor should we be willing to settle, by weight of mass opinion, for a bureaucratic economy on a low socialistic scale that will not take long to sink American policies to the level of or beneath communism.

## DEMOCRACY

Our forefathers were not only brave. I believe they were right. I believe that what they meant was that every man born had equal right to grow from scratch by way of his own power unhindered to the highest expression of himself possible to him. This of course not antagonistic but sympathetic to the growth of all men as brothers. Free emulation not imitation of the "bravest and the best" is to be expected of him. Uncommon he may and will and should become as inspiration to his fellows, not a reflection upon them, not to be resented but accepted — and in this lies the only condition of the common man's survival. So only is he intrinsic to democracy.

Persistently holding quality above quantity only as he attempts to live a superior life of his own, and to whatsoever degree in whatever case he finds it; this is his virtue in a democracy such as ours was designed to be.

Only this sense of proportion affords tranquility of spirit, in itself beauty, in either character or action. Nature is never other than serene even in a thunderstorm. The assumption of the "firm countenance, lips compressed" in denial or resentment is not known to her as it is known to civilization. Such negation by human countenance may be moral (civilization is inclined to morality) but even so not nature. Again exuberance is repose but never excess.

## THE APPEAL

Truth.

Who then is "conservative" in democracy? Would he not be the man with a sense of himself as at one with truth, seeing truth as his own love of the beautiful? "Conservative" then as he looks into nature from this inner self of his and his aims to be true to his own spirit — this is the conservative, normal to America. In this spirit beauty will ever be dear to him. Truth in every form becomes *necessary* to his spirit and the quest of appropriate form is vital to his happiness. The conservative man looking for Truth as the Beautiful, and the Beautiful as Truth. Wittingly or not, the word *beautiful* therefore is to him indissolubly associated with the word *truth*.

## FREEDOM

Liberty may be granted but freedom cannot be conferred. Freedom is from within. Notwithstanding all the abuses to which freedom is now subject — marking man down as a commercial item and cutting him off from his birthright by senseless excess and the demoralization of the profit-system — yet man may still be in love with life and find life less and less abundant for this very reason. Truth is of freedom, always safe and affirmative, therefore conservative. Truth proclaims rejection of dated minor traditions, doomed by the great Tradition. The Law of Change is truth's great "eternal." Freedom is this "great becoming."

## TRADITION

Thus to break with many of the commonly accepted ways of life is imperative to freedom. By the natural working of his own sensibility, the free mind of man in democracy is always open to the truth. Together mind and heart constitute his soul and their unity is the true protection — perhaps the only one — of his freedom.

Democratic man thus free may by his own acts enlist in the struggle for a national culture but he must himself be none the less the very hub of virtue in the circumstances. The commercializations of his era are not for him. They are not his friends. If this era is to be known as "The Sanitary Age" only, then our freedom is doomed. Democracy must die. To cultivate beauty in his society, the citizen must again see life as poetic, study the poetic principle as guide, as counselor and friend.

From within this philosophy of fundamental freedom any disorder is made manifest. Force, as Napoleon confessed, can never organize anything. Force soon renders useless our discoveries of new facilities such as those of this our Machine-age. Force reduces "progress" to affairs of mere invention, to such sub-sciences as the mere taking of things apart. Life may only be redeemed, rendered more noble, by great thought and feeling in all our art and in concise opposition to unwholesome manifestations devoid of spirit which we have long been calling tradition. "Style" taste-built is about all our evidence of culture. Unsafe because "taste" (whether old or new) is basically a matter of ignorance, seldom unless by accident on good terms with knowledge of the poetic-principle. It is necessary to know, not to taste.

PART FOUR

# THE CITY

By neglect of prophetic apprehension of the nature of the future as practical, an expedient form of centralization (no more than habituation) stands. It is now seen, at last, as foremost among American social evils, the ancient city as inheritance; not planned for modern man or his uses. Modern man has only crammed the city of his ancient brother with gadgetry and is now being demoralized by it. Scientific modern "advantages" have been his confusion and may be his defeat.

The Medieval city is still all the city he has and his gigantic financial investment in it is encouraged regardless of fate or fact. Persistently this abuse is not only by investors knowing no better but by academic authority that should know better. Enormous static, thus inherited, is perpetuated by gregarious human habit so manipulated. This giant investment in the city is an appeal to the gregarious nature of the human animal; eventually, too, to be dead-sea fruit. The urban realtor now looms as future America's most obstinate enemy, manipulating the huge barricade of urban habit in his behalf against the future of the race. Quantity is entrenched by him to put an end to quality. Life is overwhelmed, becomes an undercurrent beneath the unsafe success of mass- or quantity-production. The insolence of authority is endeavoring to substitute money for ideas.

This ominous trampling of the herd is now the traffic-problem in big-city streets. Perpetual pig-piling of enormous increasing masses of humanity, steering to and fro, rolling out to dormitory town, rolling bumper to bumper morning and evening, back and forth again and yet again, crowds packed into cubicles to work or be entertained in crowds, always invoking artificial light, crowds crowding into schools and crowds crowding university campuses, crowds crowded into brick citadels themselves the sanitary slums a grade above the old slums by sanitation; and we hear the vain boasts of science as well as of government remorselessly promoting the Crowd, more investment in crowds, always more, never less, congestion; building more roads into and out of the cities, increasing the need for parking facilities.

Meantime we boast the highest standard of living in the world, when it is only the biggest. Society finds itself helplessly committed to these excesses and pressures. Ugliness is inevitable to this inorganic, therefore senseless, waste motion of the precious life of our time become a form of involuntary homicide. So mesmerized are we by the "payoff" that any public participation in culture becomes likewise wasted. So little are we enlisted in the potential new life that belongs to America.

Thus cheated by ourselves of general culture we have little genuine architecture. Official authority being by nature more and more merely numerical is already helpless even to recognize this fact, basic as it is. However I like to believe I see continuing signs of worldwide unrest pointing to the long desired awakening, to the needed integrity of an organic architecture — the very awakening, late in the nineteenth or early in the twentieth century, foreseen by the poet Victor Hugo.


## IDEAS AND IDEALS

Our United States of America — itself a radical statement of ethical philosophy — a prophetic faith. A civic conscience is necessary to protect the new civilian freedom, promising more humanity than any promised before.

There is no individual without a point of view. It is the condition of individuality. Ideas are fountainheads! An idea is an achievement in itself; originality of thought most desirable of human qualities.

It is on this quality that the life of democracy truly depends, and on the protection it affords *its own genius*. Nor can "teamwork" — the committee-mind — ever safely be substituted for the inspirations of genius.

Any enterprise depreciating American idealism to an abject level no higher than the concept of "the common man" is either communistic or some low form of socialism that our brave progenitors feared and our friends abroad sometimes prophesy. For when the free man our forefathers conceived falls under the regime of the committee-mind, individuality is lost in the average of averages. I have never believed there is a "common man," nor does any man, not in his *own* estimation at least.

No man will ever live happily with himself or with other men under democracy unless he takes the opportunity afforded him by our nation to rise above average (the common) by his own virtue. By playing down to the idea of the common man, dogmatic political authority exploits him; and has gone far to destroy for everyone reverence for distinction and individual achievement by personal virtue and sacrifice.

So the ideal of innate aristocracy of which our forefathers dreamed is betrayed for votes in the name of democracy. But the Declaration was originally made the thesis of a solid new faith in man as individual. This man could only mean the rise from within the nation of a genuine American aristocracy of sympathy and character, a new kind of aristocracy — as I have said — *of* the man, not *on* him. Again: his not by privilege, or birth, but by virtue *earned:* aristocracy, therefore, of man's own nature: an earned benefit to his kind.


New definitions as well as new dimensions are therefore needed all down the line, including that of the now threadbare term "gentleman." Definitions now imperative in America, because danger to this nation among its neighbor-nations lies in the inferiority complexes of mediocrity exalted by the impact upon it of politics, its numerical aspects, the ubiquity of its character.


## YOUTH AND ARCHITECTURE

Our present discouragement and distortion of architecture as individual expression is alarming. Our best young men too rarely seek to be interpreters of the poetic principle, which is what an architect should be by nature. Maybe because they are no longer so born or perhaps because they are so conditioned by education; they are no longer deeply enough desired by our society to be properly rewarded.

Consider the overwhelming toll taken by the premium placed upon more "successful" professions or upon captains of industry or the persuasive salesmen of anything at all. It is "men-of-affairs" and men-of-science that are in demand; the politician rates high. All ride the tide to take what each may take of his share in society. Superior reward for inferior performance taxes heavily the young man's choice of a "career." The novice sees far greater financial chances for "security" and social standing afforded him almost anywhere else than in architecture and the arts. The true rewards in the practice of art, architecture or religious devotion are becoming dubious intangibles. Students must go into practice of architecture too cheaply — go ready-made either by rule or rote by way of some preferred educational institution and a license after spending too many years in service to a (perhaps mediocre) professional. Only then is he "licensed" to build. His experience is here reduced by inorganic regulations and rules to servitude — a requirement of his services as architect.

Therefore most of the novitiate thus "licensed" are not builders because of ability, good background or depth of character; they have no proved capacity for the long, patient experience in work which should be theirs when they start to practice. Unfortunately, it can come only later. True dedication to adequate preparation is not there; and it is not to be had "by license." Qualification is rendered not only unlikely but virtually impossible, so architects today usually lack both inspiration and integrity. A protection to which society is entitled has thus become only elimination of superior human material, an exploitation of the profession which can only be explained by their need for a continuing supply of draughtsmen. Only devotion to nature-study in the light of guiding experience under competent leadership by a qualified master can reveal to the right kind of apprentice the necessary knowledge to safeguard America from unripe or demoralizing building-performance. Instead, the young man in architecture must try every shortcut provided by the available systems of education today in order to become a tastemaker according to this name or that name as may be recommended by their "followers." But a creative artist is not to come to us by the same educational process or the same means we employ to produce a scientist, a businessman or a politician. So the story of our current architecture in any true retrospect is likely to be a sad one: architecture declining in significance and power until the tragedy of "restatement" or no statement at all worth considering becomes again "classic."

## RETROSPECT

Serious architects coming here from abroad found our culture around the beginning of the century almost completely ignorant of our own architecture or, for that matter, of any architecture except that taught by the Paris Beaux-Arts or in evidence as old "Colonial." Old Colonial derived by the English from France and by France from Medieval Italy. Italy was indebted to Greece. Greece to Egypt and Egypt to — ? (As a consequence of all this procession, see how the beam that bore the poet-builder's message to humanity down the ages has been short circuited by modern science. But only for the time being — until the true significance of the mother-art comes again clear. Every so often in history the fate of a civilization depends upon a single ray or hangs by a thread — but it has thus never yet been lost.)

The same was then true in the "liberal" arts: American society, worldly-rich, was utterly poor in art and afraid to live as itself. Fearful of being ridiculed for lacking knowledge of art, we felt much safer in buying "culture" ready-made from abroad. That is where our culture had always come from?

So, from Europe, rather than the Orient, came most of what art our people knew, and there, at top-heavy financial levels, it could, and did, buy what it wanted. America, meantime, was getting noisier, faster and uglier (the exceptions being the Louis Sullivan skyscraper and the dwellings I built on the Midwest prairie around Chicago) under the prodigious success of machine-masters. As we were, then (and not very different now), if a substitute was presented as an original — who would know? This obviously meant a consequent atrophy of our spiritual arteries.

Already educated far beyond capacity, our over-privileged society tended more and more toward some kind of servile conformity. The old box forms, stripped of ornament, were encouraged by expedient social standardizations now grown so useful. Any cliché would do. So American life was left to be quickened above the belt by any phase of art provided it was imported — Old English, Beaux-Arts or Bauhaus — or what have you? All to be subjected eventually to mass-production. Due to our skill in scientific invention, our life became more and more subject by the professional tastemakers of the country (never artists, merely artistic) to the exploitation of commonplaces.

The compulsory machinery of public education plus the real-estate "developer" (and we have now government housing not to mention the public "service" corporation) all contributed to the degradation of the beauty America promised.

Add a vast and growing bureaucracy to this, and the natural result of machine politics was the man more and more a machine. Our biggest machine became not the corporations of big industry, but incorporated government, and biggest of all, the machinery of education.

In general (of necessity) machinery feeds and thrives on quantity production. So our society became subject to the influence of profit-minded industries (and what other kind of industry have we?).

"Profit-minded" meant, first and foremost, *quantity*-minded. Owing to endless machine invention and production, the reproduction of the substitute was easily accepted.

Even in 1893 art was servile to "big business." It is now easy to see how architecture, art (and religion, too) become subservient to business in order to survive. The university not much above the level of a trade school or business college (business has now made a college degree a virtual requirement); and higher education is largely a cultural liability backed by big American executives themselves.

Though often sensitive, sensible (occasionally mature), these money-magnates seldom allowed themselves any show of feeling for the cultivation of beauty. To give to beauty more than a casual look or gesture, to give any extensive (or expensive) consideration to the "beautification" of even their own business world — though it is now at last increasing — would have seemed, to most of them, weak — if not waste motion.

The machine thus magnified became Moloch, dominant as quantity factor. So, instead of raising the quality, it increased only the *size*, of the standard of living of our society, inevitably reducing the value of the man himself.

Any honest, intelligent analysis of our situation will show that, with rare exceptions, money must talk, take over, and decide even these matters of the soul. Success breeds success, but where success breeds excess maintained by some form of advertising, the end is unpleasant to see. Advertising, subsidized by government — at public expense — is really our most distinguished form of art, and grows rank and noxious as any weed.

## TECHNOLOGY AGAIN

Why did the manpower and technology of the haphazard uprisings of building that characterize our big cities almost entirely escape the essential hand of the creative artist-architect? Wherever and how did he ever manage to survive? His apparent contribution to American life is still small and continually ignored by the business-administration of art by "efficient" plan factories.

Novelty seems always to be a good form of advertising a substitute. And superficial architecture is based upon just such a temporary novel appeal, and thus upon "taste." Organic architecture cannot have the automatic advantage attaching to the substitute. So it has not been able to qualify much this appalling drift toward expedient conformity. It is hard to realize that until recently organic architecture was comparatively unknown to our people.

*To what extent is the bureaucrat to determine the culture of our civilization?* The "insolence of office" thrives upon conformity. See now the distortion of our intrinsic social purpose by experts and specialists and the encouragement of mediocrity by mass-education. With the inspiration of great art unheeded, where is the check to deterioration? Are architecture and art simply to fade out with religion?

Still to be discovered as a devoted son of culture is the inspired architect, the public servant who, if appreciated and used, could express the quality of depth and validity in the human values of our society, enabling us to qualify this ruthless imposition of quantity over quality. The artist-architect will be a man inspired by love of the nature of Nature, knowing that man is not made for architecture; architecture is made for man. He will see the practice of architecture never as a business but always religiously as basic to the welfare and culture of humanity as, at its best, it ever has been. And we must recognize the creative architect as poet and interpreter of life. We have only to consider what he has done and where he has been in every true culture of all time to see how important this son of culture is to our own future as a nation. By way of a growing art chiefly comes the culture that fertilizes society, by fructifying the individual and enabling men to call their lives their own. This enrichment of life is the cause of Architecture, as I see it.

Both abroad and at home I find that good minds still doubt the consequences of such all-out commercialism as characterizes our life and threatens human interest here in America. Yet, wholesale mechanization now seems a matter of course; technology and science menace the exuberance, the richness, of life expression and help to fashion it into a monotonous Style without human scale or significance.

The machine as a tool now is inevitable to human joy and comfort, and originals must have, in themselves, properties essential to the proper use of our machine-powers. But, machined-shapes are no *substitute* for architectural form, nor is the machine itself a form-giver or interpreter.

## SALVATION

If our American engineers had had more sense of organic architecture in their systems and the architects more sense of organic engineering, the fate of our modernization of medievality would not be so tragic. Full-scale planning, afresh, might have saved city life for another half-century, or more.

The primitive ideals of centralization are now largely self-defeating. Human crucifixion by verticality on the now static checkerboard of the old city is pattern already in agony; yet for lack of any organic planning it is going on and on — not living, but rather hanging by its eyebrows from its nervous system.

1955.   HAROLD C. PRICE, JR. HOUSE, BARTLESVILLE, OKLAHOMA

LIVING ROOM

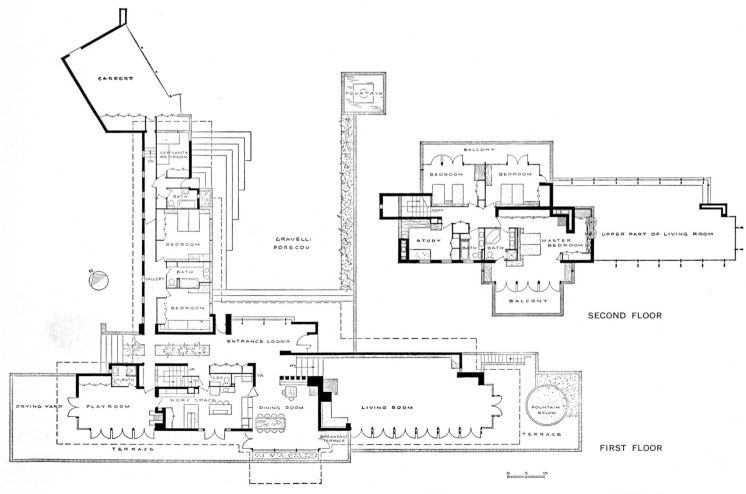

FIRST FLOOR

SECOND FLOOR

1955.  HAROLD C. PRICE, JR. HOUSE, BARTLESVILLE, OKLAHOMA

MASTER BEDROOM

VIEW FROM THE SOUTH. LIVING ROOM TERRACE IN FOREGROUND, RIGHT.

1953-56. H. C. PRICE COMPANY TOWER, BARTLESVILLE, OKLAHOMA. "THE TREE THAT ESCAPED THE CROWDED FOREST. WINNING DOMINANCE AT NO MAN'S EXPENSE BUT THEIR OWN, THE PRICE COMPANY ENJOYS ALL THERE IS TO BE HAD THROUGH COMPLETE USE OF PREFERRED, CONVENIENT, COMPACT SPACE IN OPEN SKY. (THIS TYPE OF SHELTERED-GLASS TOWER I FIRST DESIGNED IN 1924 FOR CHICAGO AND IN 1929 FOR ST. MARK'S-IN-THE-BOUWERIE IN NEW YORK.)"

1955.   HAROLD C. PRICE HOUSE, PHOENIX, ARIZONA

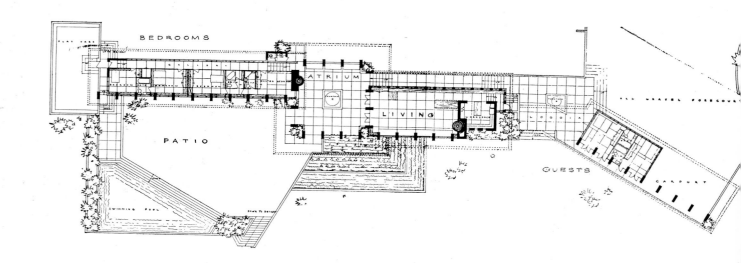

ATRIUM, OPEN ON ALL SIDES TO THE SKY, CONNECTS LIVING ROOM AND BEDROOM WINGS. THE GREAT ROOFS HOVER LIGHTLY OVER THE HOUSE AFFORDING THE UNIQUE SENSE OF SHELTER, LIGHT, AND SOFT SHADOW CHARACTERISTIC OF ORGANIC ARCHITECTURE

LIVING ROOM, VIEW TOWARD DINING AREA AND FIREPLACE

VIEW THROUGH LIVING ROOM TOWARD ENTRY FROM ATRIUM

1955.   HAROLD C. PRICE HOUSE, PHOENIX, ARIZONA

Well-meaning ignorance and greed habitual add story to story, congestion to congestion, in order for the landlord to "pay off." Landlordism, now a disease of our profit-system, fights skyscraper with skyscraper. The frantic attempt to salvage urban investment destroys all human values and tries to make the human creature like it. The upended street is the invention that made possible this attempt to cage human beings.

Our oversized mobiles with non-mobile shapes — sheer excess — squared off, squared up platforms, swallowing four wheels, barge between trucks scaled more to the railroads than to city streets; all making menace constant and driving a hazard. Add to this the mortgage on our American landscape forged and fore-closed by the pole-and-wire men — and the citizen himself is condemned; on the road but headed for bankruptcy.

Owing to demolition of human values, saturation is not far away. Life itself is now distorted out of proportion, out of perspective. Everywhere in the city the citizen is treated by service itself as a servant. Subject to this universal back-firing of modern "advantages," now featured and practiced like a tax levied upon him, he is becoming a piece of machinery himself, his city a vast urban garage.

Fission of the atom might eventually prove the logical conclusion to his insoluble traffic problem created by human cupidity plus stupidity. Elimination of our badly overgrown cities, if only to release man from this growing universal bondage, would be merciful? Organic planning by way of organic architecture would be liberation. By decentralization. The forces that will eventually secure this planning are meantime at work. Why do we not work with them? The architect as more engineer and the engineer as more architect could by now have had man's liberation well under way.

First principles of organic architecture bring much light upon a new type of agrarian-urban planning. But even without benefit of such planning, the building of the new city is going on. Inevitable undercurrents beneath the old city life are taking both city and country apart. To bring them back together again in *humane* proportion is not the work of science or commerce; it requires the vision of the architect in love with architecture.

Everywhere pushed to extremes, the abuses of machine-power, the gigantic property interests cast ominous shadows upon defenseless *human* interests.

The character of "modern" citizenship is more a hangover from the animal than ever — and yet "humanity begins where the animal leaves off"? Yes. But the urbanite seems willing not only to go in to be pig-piled flat, but now to be pig-piled up on end. The realtor-landlord and the landlord-realtor, prime movers of present urban centralization, take him up and take him down; in and out, to and fro goes the hapless victim, until he is finally "taken over." By what? And how?

His coming emancipation is what should matter most to him now, notwithstanding his habituate embrace of deadly factual routine. His essential dignity remains only in his intelligent sense of himself. Fortunately for him he is learning to see Architecture as basic element of his civilization, and to understand that his birthright lies in that higher nature to which, for the sake not merely of his survival but of his happiness, he aspires. Decentralization and organic reintegration of his city is chiefly an affair of architecture.

## ORGANIC CHARACTERISTICS

Quiet mass-outlines extended upon the ground levels in becoming human proportions throughout: an appropriate new use of materials old and new: these characterized the early straight-line, flat-plane dwellings built by myself — happily and with great hope — on the midwest prairie I loved, beginning 1893. Buildings creating a free, new phase of horizontality were also characteristic of the capacity of our new tool, the machine; and a new sense of human scale.

New-old philosophy had come to the rescue, soon afforded new freedoms in design. The plan grew more beneficial to human life. Eventually to do so universally. These initial buildings were made to declare and express the affinity not only of man's life to his ground, but of the ground to the nature of the man who lived upon it. They showed how the inevitable order of the machine was better fitted as a tool to build these new buildings than any means ever known. But this revelation could not have been made under the old codes, nor could it have come alive under the rules of the old classic or medieval order.

Box-frame architecture, being set up on every hand as the urban ideal, also constituting the respectability of our "more educated" villagers. These standard lines of dreary human cages, with flat lids or none visible, that stretched for miles and miles were indistinguishably serving to live in, to live by; to learn in, to play in. The steeple marked the box to pray in, the dome the box to rule in.

## THE NEW CLICHE

Now, latest in the succession of habituated boxation is the open box with glassified poster-facade standing on urban streets from Chicago to New York — representing contagion? Box to box, boxes within the box, framed by steel from the outside in, has long been the traditional form of building; but if this boxation is to continue, why call it modern architecture? We know better. What we now need is not more nineteenth century architecture of this type. Past the middle of the twentieth century, we are at last ready for twentieth century architecture.

As for novelty, everybody is learning to know that almost all sensationalism is good advertising and may be made to serve commerce. But there is neither architecture nor artistry in any of it; only a low level of invention, at best. Prolixity bred to propinquity, these mantraps seem to express the herd ideal spread by way of advertising, and accepted by man's own default. We see here the breakdown, owing to man's lack of faith in himself, of our national ideal: the sovereignty of the individual. We see here the triumph of conformity, man the individual now man as termite.

Integrity of *principle* is lacking in all this, but perhaps the self-immolating confusion called "modern architecture" is only a preliminary skirmish on the way to true modernity. Probably as old style, restyled; novel, not new, but on the whole better than the usual collection of older eclecticisms known as "the classic."

Knowledge that could retrieve from imitation the original effects of organic architecture is not forthcoming from contemporary graduates of our colleges.

With no principle or ethical performance, these mere effects are taken as a new style, one to be copied, so the cliché.

Managed publicity in newsprint, in magazines and on the air is for architects instead of architecture, and the standardized architectural schooling in our universities, their curriculum a mere run-around, seems designed to go along with formulas now being substituted for performance. Much of the criticism we know aids, if indeed it is not inspired by, this expediency. Here is one reason why our "modern architecture" grows in platitude and volume while decreasing in sensitive, imaginative significance. The art of building steadily diminishes in spiritual character by the brainwashing architects receive as education. "Practice makes perfect," only if practice be right. But if the practice be wrong?

Genuine expressions as essence of the great art itself cannot be taught or imitated. Nor can they in any way be forced. If the quality of vision we call inspiration is lacking, all is lacking; and inspiration comes in its own good time in its own way, from within — comes only when all is ready, and usually must wait.

Great art has always, at first, been controversial. Now that our means of communication have multiplied, how much more so today? Any moot point soon becomes every man's controversy. Specialists in controversy, numerous and vociferous, sprout on every branch. And the pressure toward conformity leaves young minds weak with the uncertainty that cleaves, for reassurance, to the static in some form.

Resemblances are mistaken for influences. Comparisons have been made odious where comparison should, except as insult, hardly exist. Minds imbued by the necessity of truth, uttering truths independently of each other and capable of learning by analysis instead of comparison are still few. Scholarly appraisals? Only rarely are they much above the level of gossip. So, up comes comparison, to compare organic architecture to the Crystal Palace of London, for instance — Horatio Greenough, *Art Nouveau,* Emerson, Whitman, Sullivan, Coleridge, Thoreau, etc.

Those adversaries of truth who claim its discovery are invariably traitorous. Contemporary criticism is mostly posture, at the back door or at best side entrance, therefore a mere guess as to what the affair really looked like from the front. Every now and then one of the so-dedicated writes a book about a book written by a man who did the same, to win the "take away" prize in this game; never actually to be won because it was lost before it started.

## INFLUENCES AND INFERENCES

To cut ambiguity short: there never was exterior influence upon my work, either foreign or native, other than that of Lieber Meister, Dankmar Adler and John Roebling, Whitman and Emerson, and the great poets worldwide. My work is original not only in fact but in spiritual fiber. No practice by any European architect to this day has influenced mine in the least.

As for the Incas, the Mayans, even the Japanese — all were to me but splendid confirmation. Some of our own critics could be appreciated —Lewis Mumford (*Sticks and Stones*), early Russell Hitchcock, Montgomery Schuyler and a few others.

While admiring Henry Hobson Richardson, I instinctively disliked his patron Henry Adams as our most accomplished (therefore most dangerous) promoter of eclecticism. I believed Adams, Boston Brahmin, would dislike Louis Sullivan and Walt Whitman. His frame of reference was never theirs, or mine. My enthusiasm for "sermons in stones and books in running brooks" was not "fascination frantic for ruins romantic — when sufficiently decayed."

At that early day I was thrilled by Mayan, Inca and Egyptian remains, loved the Byzantine. The Persian fire-domed, fire-backed structures were beautiful to me. But never anything Greek except the sculpture and the Greek vase — the reward of their persistence in search of the elegant solution. My search was more for the exception that went to prove the rule, than for the rule itself.

As for inspiration from human nature, there were Laotze, Jesus, Dante, Beethoven, Bach, Vivaldi, Palestrina, Mozart. Shakespeare was in my pocket for the many years I rode the morning train to Chicago. I learned, too, from William Blake (all of his work I read), Goethe, Wordsworth, Dr. Johnson, Carlyle (*Sartor Resartus* at the age of fourteen), George Meredith, Victor Hugo, Voltaire, Rousseau, Cervantes, Nietzsche, Unamuno, Heraclitus, Aristotle, Aristophanes.

I loved the Byzantine of San Sophia — a true dome in contrast to Michelangelo's bastard. I loved the great Momoyama period in Japanese painting and the later Ukiyoe as I found it in the woodblock prints of the periods. These prints I collected with extravagant devotion and shameful avidity, and sat long at the inspiring series of Hokusai and Hiroshige; learned much from Korin, Kenzan, Sotatz and always the primitives. The Ukiyoe and the Momoyama, Japanese architecture and gardening, confirmed my own feeling for my work and delighted me, as did Japanese civilization which seemed so freshly and completely of the soil, organic.

Gothic soared for me, too; but seldom if ever the Renaissance in architecture, outside the original contributions of the Italians. I read, being a minister's son, much of the Bible; and inhabited, now and then, all the great museums of the world, from America to London, across the globe to Tokyo.

I read and respected many of our own poets and philosophers, among them: Emerson, Thoreau, Melville, William James, Charles Beard, John Dewey, Mark Twain, our supreme humorist-story-teller; especially the giver of the new religion of democracy, Walt Whitman. I cared little for the great pragmatists in philosophy and less for the Greek sophists. Historicism always seemed equivocal to me; the best of the histories Gibbon's *Rome;* my respect for Frederick Froebel always high owing to my mother's kindergarten table. Soon I turned away from the Greek abstraction via Oxford or elsewhere. Of all the fine arts, music it was that I could not live without, and — as taught by my father (the symphony an edifice of sound) — found in it sympathetic parallel to architecture. Beethoven, and Bach too, were princely architects in my spiritual realm.

I liked Beethoven's great disciple, Brahms. Italy was to me and is still so ever the beating heart of art creative, manifest in Vivaldi, the Italian troubadours and Palestrina. They came along with Giotto, Mantegna, Leonardo, etc.

My mother taught me, in my childhood as described, the kindergarten "gifts" of Frederick Froebel — a true philosopher. At the age of eleven I was confided by my mother to her brother, my uncle James, on the farm in "the Valley" to practice both edifice and gifts as I might, and did. Never a thought in politics as other than profane until I was past fifty-five.

## WISDOM

Again: I found repeatedly confirmed that the inferior mind not only learns by comparison, but loosely confers its superlatives, while the superior mind which learns by analysis refrains from superlatives. I have learned about architecture by root, by world-wide travel and by incessant experiment and experience in the study of nature. In the midst of sensible experiment based always upon preliminary experiments, I never had the courage to lie. Meantime I lived with all the expressions of beauty I could see. And all those that I could acquire and use for study and enjoyment I acquired as my library, but living with them all as I might. I never had much respect for the collector's mind.

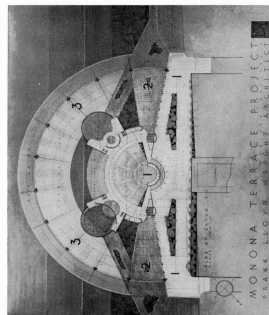

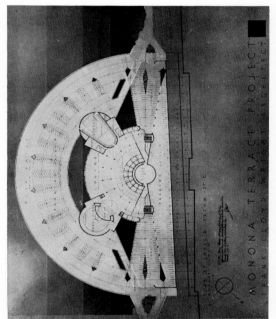

1955. MONONA TERRACE PROJECT, MADISON, WISCONSIN. PLAN ON RIGHT SHOWS: 1) CIVIC CENTER AND AUDITORIUM AND PARKING. 2) ADDITIONAL PARKING, MUNICIPAL BOAT HOUSES AND MUSEUM AND THEATRE AREAS ABOVE. 3) EXTENDED PARKING FACILITIES. THE CIVIC GARDENS ABOVE, WHICH APPLY TO ALL THREE. FINALLY THERE ARE TWO PROJECTED SKYSCRAPERS FOR REVENUE. THE PLAN ON LEFT SHOWS EXTENSION OF BALCONY OF TERRACE ON BEYOND SHORE LINE. THE COMPLETED SCHEME INCLUDES PARKING FOR MORE THAN 3,500 CARS, AUDITORIUM AND CIVIC CENTER BUILDINGS, TOGETHER WITH THE PUBLIC PLEASURE GARDENS, BOATHOUSES, THE LAKE DRIVE—WEDDING THE CITY OF MADISON TO BEAUTIFUL LAKE MONONA

209

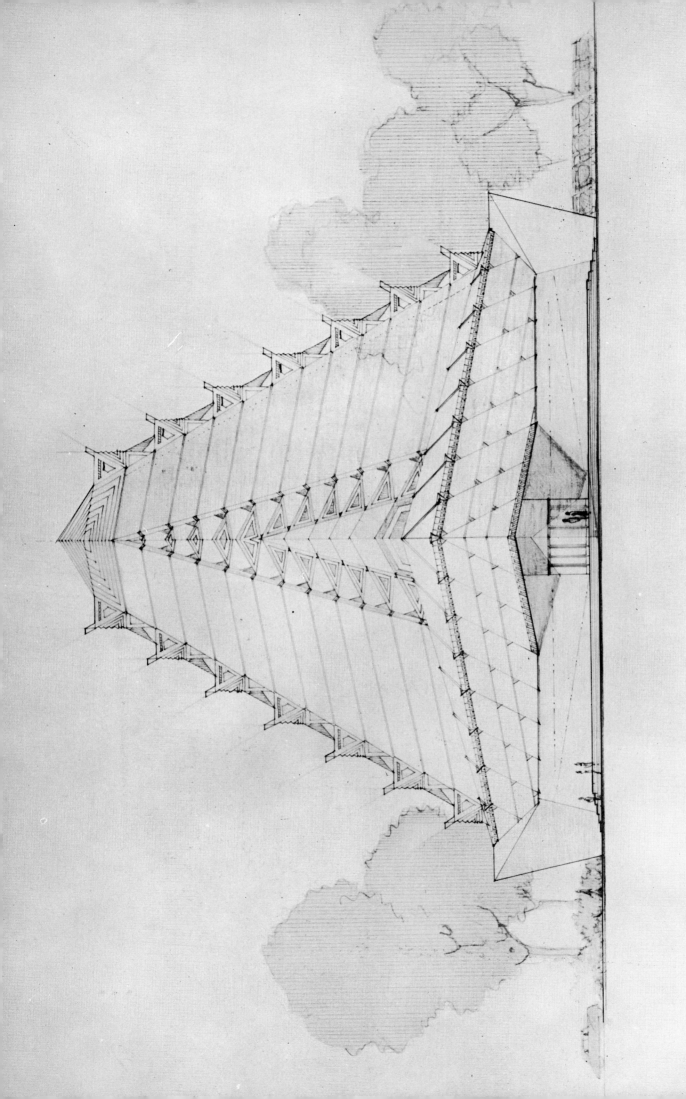

1954. BETH SHOLEM SYNAGOGUE, PHILADELPHIA, PENNSYLVANIA
"WE WANT TO BUILD AN AMERICAN SYNAGOGUE FOR JEWS TO
WORSHIP IN. WE WANT TO CREATE THE KIND OF BUILDING IN
WHICH PEOPLE, ON ENTERING IT, WILL FEEL AS IF THEY WERE
RESTING IN THE HANDS OF GOD."

SECTION THROUGH—PLASTIC, CONCRETE AND COPPER CONSTRUCTION —CONGREGATION ABOVE, CHAPEL AND LOUNGES BELOW, ENTRANCE. SEVEN-BRANCHED CANDLESTICKS, MENORAHS, ARE SET UPON ITS THREE GREAT RIDGES

1954. BETH SHOLEM SYNAGOGUE, PHILADELPHIA, PENNSYLVANIA—NIGHT VIEW

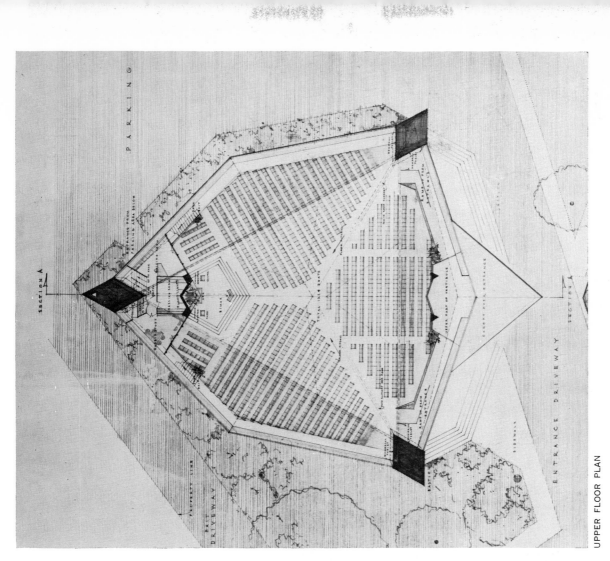

UPPER FLOOR PLAN

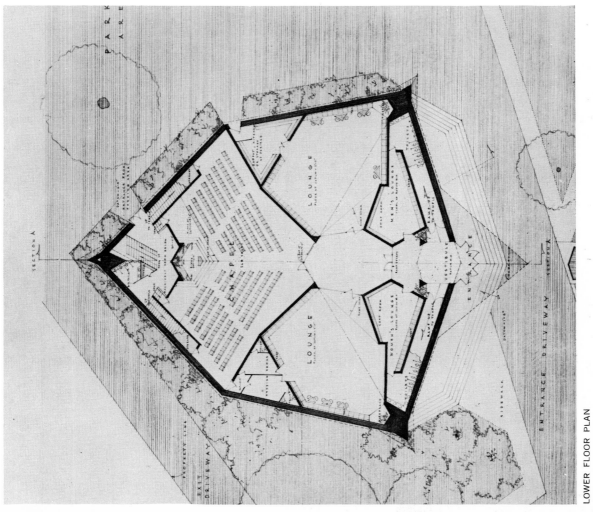

LOWER FLOOR PLAN

213

1956. THE NEW SPORTS PAVILION (FOR RACETRACK AND OTHER SPORTS) BELMONT AND AQUEDUCT, NEW YORK. A MASSIVE SLAB, WITH FOUR LEVELS REACHED BY TWELVE OR SIXTEEN ESCALATORS (DEPENDING ON SIZE OF STAND), COVERED BY A TRANSLUCENT PLASTIC ROOF, SUSPENDED ON A LACEWORK OF SLENDER TENSILE STEEL CABLES. THERE WILL BE NO PILLARS OF ANY KIND, AFFORDING TOTAL VISIBILITY FOR 65,000 OR 80,000 PEOPLE; PARKING SPACE FOR FROM 3,500 TO 5,000 CARS, AGAIN DEPENDING ON THE SIZE OF THE STRUCTURE. TWO TALL TOWERS SITUATED AT ENDS OF STANDS ARE TO BE BANKED WITH FLOODLIGHTS CAPABLE OF LIGHTING THE ENTIRE STRUCTURE, THE ILLUMINATION POURING THROUGH THE TRANSLUCENT ROOF. WATER PIPES EMBEDDED IN THE FLOORS AT THE VARIOUS LEVELS WILL CARRY HOT WATER TO WARM THE STRUCTURE IN COLD WEATHER. ALL WAGERING FACILITIES, RESTAURANTS, SNACK BARS AND REST ROOMS WILL BE DIRECTLY UNDER EACH BANK OF SEATS OR BOXES ON FOUR LEVELS, WITH EASY ACCESS FROM THE SEATS, ARRANGED TO ELIMINATE LONG QUEUES. "A STRUCTURE THAT IS ORGANIC IN CHARACTER, AND THIS PRINCIPLE CAN BE APPLIED, AND ULTIMATELY MUST BE, TO EVERY HUMAN ENDEAVOR ARCHITECTURALLY."

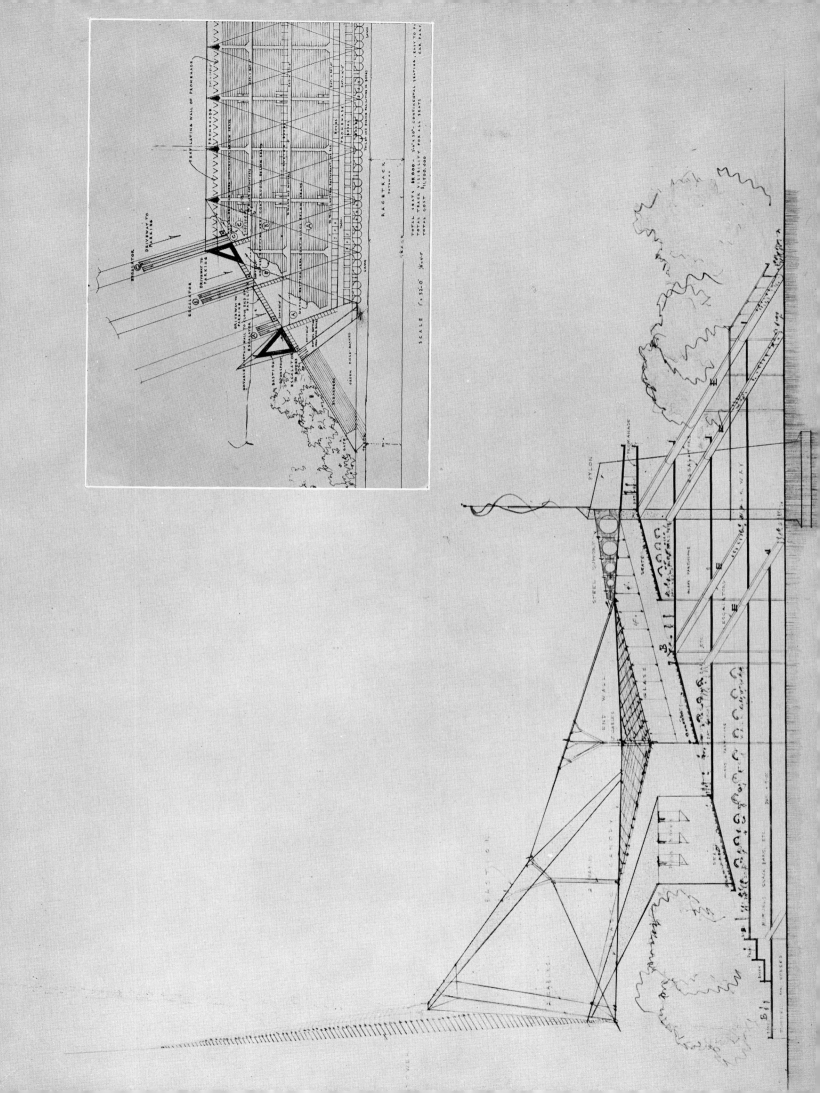

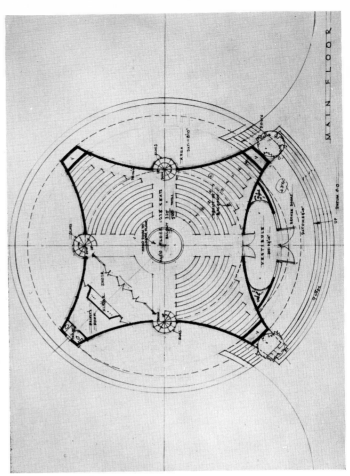

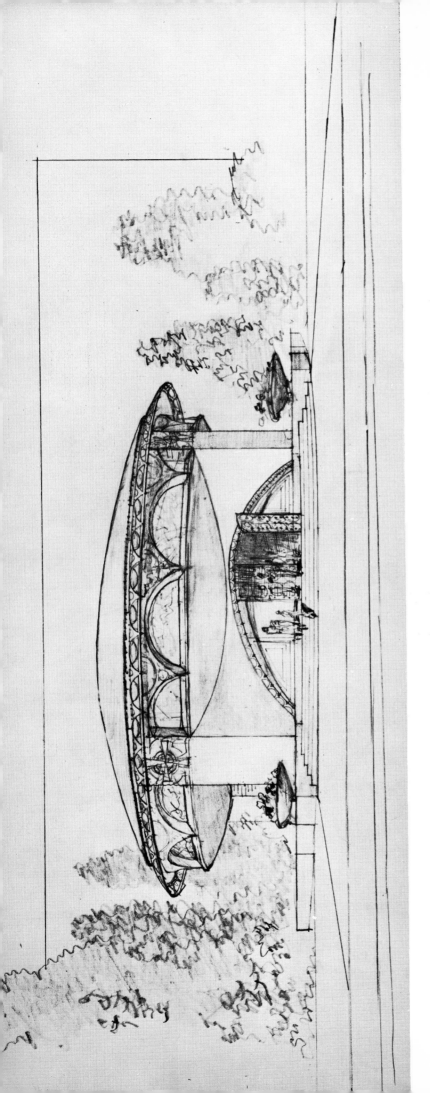

MAIN FLOOR

1956.  PROJECT, GREEK ORTHODOX CHURCH, MILWAUKEE, WISCONSIN

# BOOK TWO
## THE NEW ARCHITECTURE

# PART ONE
## PRINCIPLES

# I. THE EARTH LINE

At last we come to the analysis of the principles that became so solidly basic to my sense and practice of architecture. How do these principles, now beginning to be recognized as the centerline of American democracy, work?

PRINCIPLE ONE: KINSHIP OF BUILDING TO GROUND. This basic inevitability in organic architecture entails an entirely new sense of proportion. The human figure appeared to me, about 1893 or earlier, as the true *human* scale of architecture. Buildings I myself then designed and built — Midwest — seemed, by means of this new scale, to belong to man and at the moment especially as he lived on rolling Western prairie. Soon I had occasion to observe that every inch of height there on the prairie was exaggerated. All breadths fell short. So in breadth, length, height and weight, these buildings belonged to the prairie just as the human being himself belonged to it with his gift of speed. The term "streamlined" as my own expression was then and there born.

As result, the new buildings were rational: low, swift and clean, and were studiously adapted to machine methods. The quiet, intuitional, horizontal line (it will always be the line of human tenure on this earth) was thus humanly interpreted and suited to modern machine-performance. Machine-methods and these new streamlined, flat-plane effects first appeared together in our American architecture as expression of new ways to reach true objectives in building. The main objective was gracious appropriation of the art of architecture itself to the Time, the Place, and Modern Man.

What now is organic "design"? Design appropriate to modern tools, the machine, and this new human scale. Thus, design was opportune, and well within the architect's creative hand if his mind was receptive to these relatively new values: moving perception at this time with reverential spirit toward the understanding of the "nature of nature." The nature of the machine, studied by experiment and basically used in structural design, was still to be limited to a tool, and proved to be a powerful new medium of expression. Buildings before long were evidencing beautiful simplicity, a fresh exuberance of countenance. Originality.

Never did I allow the machine to become "motif" — always machine for man and never man for the machine. Every since, in organic architecture I have used the machine and evolved a system of building from the inside out, always according to the nature of both man and machine — as I could see it — avoiding the passing aspects now characteristic of urban architecture. The machine I found a better means to broaden the humane interest in modern architecture. Nor, in point of style, have I once looked upon the machine as in itself an end, either in planning or building or style. Quantity has never superseded quality.

## THE MODULAR OF THE KINDERGARTEN TABLE

Kindergarten training, as I have shown, proved an unforeseen asset: for one thing, because later all my planning was devised on a properly proportional unit system. I found this would keep all to scale, ensure consistent proportion throughout the edifice, large or small, which thus became — like tapestry — a consistent fabric woven of interdependent, related units, however various.

So from the very first this system of "fabrication" was applied to planning even in minor buildings. Later, I found technological advantages when this system was applied to heights. In elevation, therefore, soon came the vertical module as experience might dictate. All this was very much like laying warp on the loom. The woof (substance) was practically the same as if stretched upon this predetermined warp. This basic practice has proved indispensable and good machine technique must yield its advantages. Invariably it appears in organic architecture as visible feature in the fabric of the design — insuring unity of proportion. The harmony of texture is thus, with the scale of all parts, within the complete ensemble.

## II. IMPULSE TO GROW

PRINCIPLE TWO: DECENTRALIZATION. The time for more individual spaciousness was long past due. 1893. I saw urban-decentralization as inevitable because a growing necessity, seeking more space everywhere, by whatever steps or stages it was obtainable. Space, short of breath, was suffocating in an airless situation, a shameful imposition upon free American life. Then, as now, the popular realtor with his "lot" was enemy of space; he was usually busy adding limitation to limitation, rounding up the herd and exploiting the ground for quick profit.

Indigestible competition, thus added to the big city, despoiled the villages. Over-extended verticality then congested to hold the profits of congestion was added to the congestion already fashioned on the ground.

To offset the senselessness of this inhuman act, I prepared the Broadacre City models at Taliesin in 1932. The models proposed a new space concept in social usage for individual and community building. But the whole establishment was laid out in accordance with the conditions of land tenure already in effect. Though the centers were kept, a new system of subdivision was proposed.

Later, this model of the broader use of ground for a new idea of a new city was carefully studied in detail in a series of smaller tributary models, all as described in *When Democracy Builds,* a book I later wrote on the suggestion of Robert Hutchins. Buildings, roads, planting, habitation, cultivation, decoration, all became as architectural as they were in Umbria in Italy in the Middle Ages; qualities of ancient sort in modern form for modern times, considered in terms of modern humane utility. Thus broadened, the view of architecture as basic now in service to society came as relief and gave a preview of primary form facing the law of the changes inevitable.

Therefore quantity — the machine source — was in no way, nor anywhere, at any time, to be used to hinder the quality of new resources for human profit and delight in living. Living was to be a quality of man's own spirit.

Science, the great practical resource, had proceeded to date itself and magnify the potential sacrifice of man as menial, now wholesale destruction of democracy. Congested in cities by continually bigger mechanical means to avoid labor, man was to be given a new freedom. The ground plan of Broadacre City was bound together in advantageous, interactive relationship to the new resources of human life under protected freedom, our own if only we would reach out and take it.

Convenient, inspiring continuity appeared in this plan for a new community (still called a city), inevitable to the survival of human individuality. But I have learned that a new pattern can never be made out of the old one: only palliation is possible — and is soon inefficient. These initial Broadacre City models, still to be seen at Taliesin, were exhibited at Rockefeller Center, New York, 1934, and many times since, elsewhere in our country and abroad. Notwithstanding the A.I.A. and the critics, this complete group-model, new in concept and pattern, showing the new life of agrarian-urbanism and urbanized-agrarianism, virtually the wedding of city and country, reappeared to travel around the world in the exhibition "Sixty Years of Living Architecture." After being shown in Philadelphia, Florence, Paris Beaux-Arts (where I was told this was the only one-man exhibition since the one accorded to James McNeill Whistler), Zurich Art Institute, Munich Art Palace, Rotterdam Civic Center, University of Mexico, it returned to a special exhibition building in New York City, and later to a special extension of Olive Hill in Los Angeles by the Municipal Art Society.

## III. CHARACTER IS A NATURAL

THREE: Appropriate "character" is inevitable to all architecture if organic. Significance of any building would clearly express its objective, its purpose — whether store, apartment building, bank, church, hotel or pie-club, factory, circus or school. Fundamental requirement, this should apply to all building, in ground-planning and, especially, relative to human life and its site. This means sane appropriation of imaginative design to specific human purposes, by the natural use of nature-materials or synthetics, and appropriate methods of construction. Our new resources already evolved by science, especially glass and steel wrought by the machine, are bound continually to develop new forms. Continually new ways and shapes of building will continue to give fresh character and true significance to all modern structure.

Poetic tranquility instead of a more deadly "efficiency," should be the consequence in the art of Building: concordant, sane, exuberant, and appropriate to purpose. Durable, serviceable, economical. Beautiful. In the ever-changing circumstances of complex modern existence all this is not too easy to accomplish and the extent of these evolving changes may not yet be fully seen but as architects we may thus reconstitute architecture in our hearts and minds and act to re-write our dated "codes" and refrain from disfiguring our American landscape by buildings or "service" systems.

## IV. TENUITY PLUS CONTINUITY

FOUR: Completely new character by these simple means came to architecture; came to view, not by haphazard use, but by organic interpretation, of steel and glass. Steel gave rise to a new property: I call it *tenuity*. Tenuity is simply a matter of tension (pull), something never before known in the architecture of this world. No building could withstand a pull. Push it you might and it would stay together but pull on it and it would fall apart. With tensile strength of steel, this pull permits free use of the cantilever, a projectile and tensile at the same time, in building-design. The outstretched arm with its hand (with its drooping fingers for walls) is a cantilever. So is the branch of a tree.

The cantilever is essentially steel at its most economical level of use. The principle of the cantilever in architecture develops tenuity as a wholly new human expression, a means, too, of placing all loads over central supports, thereby balancing extended load against opposite extended load. This brought into architecture for the first time another principle in construction — I call it *continuity* — a property which may be seen as a new, elastic, cohesive *stability*. The creative architect finds here a marvelous new inspiration in design. A new freedom involving far wider spacings of more slender supports. Thus architecture arrived at construction from within outward rather than from outside inward; much heightening and lightening of proportions throughout all building is now economical and natural, space extended and utilized in a more liberal planning than the ancients could ever have dreamed of. This is now prime characteristic of the new architecture called organic.

Rigid box shapes, outsides steel-framed, belong strictly to the nineteenth century. They cannot be twentieth century architecture. Support at rigid corners becomes mere obstruction: corners themselves now insignificant become extravagant waste, mere accents of enclosure. Construction lightened by means of cantilevered steel in tension, makes continuity a most valuable characteristic of architectural enlightenment. Our new architectural freedom now lies within this province. In the character of this new circumstance buildings now may proceed *from within outward*: Because push or pull may be integral to building design.

## V. THE THIRD DIMENSION: INTERPRETATION

FIVE: To sum up, organic architecture sees the third dimension never as weight or mere thickness but always as *depth*. Depth an element of space; the third (or thickness) dimension transformed to a *space* dimension. A penetration of the inner depths of space in spaciousness becomes architectural and valid motif in design. With this concept of depth interpenetrating depths comes flowering a freedom in design which architects have never known before but which they may now employ in their designs as a true liberation of life and light within walls; a new structural integrity; outside coming in; and the space within, to be lived in, going out. Space outside becomes a natural part of space *within* the building. All building design thus actually becomes four-dimensional and renders more static than ever the two-dimensional effects of the old static post and girder, beam and box frame type of construction, however novel they seem to be made. Walls are now apparent more as humanized screens. They do define and differentiate, but never confine or obliterate space. A new sense of reality in building construction has arrived.

Now a new liberation may be the natural consequence in every building exterior. The first conscious expression of which I know in modern architecture of this *new reality* — the "space within to be lived in" — was Unity Temple in Oak Park. True harmony and economic elements of beauty were consciously planned and belong to this new sense of space-within. The age-old philosophy of Laotze is alive in architecture. In every part of the building freedom is active. Space the basic element in architectural design.

This affirmation, due to the new sense of "the space within" as reality, came from the original affirmative negation (the great protestant) 1904, the Larkin Building of Buffalo — now demolished. Here came the poetic principle of freedom itself as a new revelation in architecture. This new freedom that was first consciously demonstrated in Unity Temple, Oak Park (1906) as written in 1927 for AN AUTOBIOGRAPHY. With this new principle at work in our American architecture came a new sense of style as innate. A quality natural to the act and art of modern habitation: no longer applied by "taste." (Again: "Such as the life is, such is the form" — Coleridge gives us perhaps a better slogan than Form Follows Function.) For Americans as for all shades and shapes of human beings everywhere "style" becomes generic: poetic expression of character. Style is intrinsic — or it is false. As a characteristic of "the space within to be lived in" — the life of style is perpetually fresh.


## VI. SPACE

SIX: Space, elemental to architecture, has now found architectural expression. Glass: air in air, to keep air out or keep it in. Steel, a strand slight and strong as the thread of the spider spinning, is able now to span extraordinary spaces. By new products of technology and increased inventive ingenuity in applying them to building-construction many superlative new space-forms have already come alive: and, because of them, more continually in sight. Some as a matter of course will be novel but insignificant; some will be significant and really new. But more important, modern building becomes the solid creative art which the poetic principle can release and develop. Noble, vital, exuberant forms are already here. Democracy awakes to a more spiritual expression. Indigenous culture will now awaken. Properly focused upon needs of twentieth century life, new uses of livable space will continually evolve, improved; more exuberant and serene. A new security and a new tranquility. Enlightened enjoyment of fresh beauty is here or due. As for the future: encouraging to me are the many letters, coming continually, country-wide, from teen-agers now in high school, asking for help with the term theses they have chosen to write upon organic architecture. This widening of the awareness of the coming generation's interest in architecture can only mean a new American architecture. When these youngsters become fathers and mothers, say a generation hence, they are going to demand appropriate space-homes on these modern terms. We will soon see the house as a work of art and because of its intrinsic beauty more a home than ever.

## VII. FORM

SEVEN: Anyone anything of an architect will never be content to design a building merely (or chiefly) for the picture it makes — any more than a man would buy a horse merely by its color. What kind of intellect must the critic have who seeing a building judges it by "the look of it," ignorant of the nature of its construction?

For the first time in 500 years a sense of architectural form appears as a new spiritual integrity.

Heavy walls, senseless overheads and overloads of every sort, vanish — let us be glad. Light and thin walls may now depend from cantilever slabs supported from the interior on shallow, dry-wall footings, walls themselves becoming slender screens, entirely independent of use as support. Centralized supports may stand isolated, balancing load against load — seen not as walls at all, but as integral pattern; walls may be slender suspension from point to point, in fascinating pendant forms. In general, structure now becomes an affair from the inside outward instead of from the outside inward. Various geometrical forms (circular especially) in planning structure become more economical than the square of the box. Building loads may be suspended, suspension supported by slender, isolated uprights. Glass or light plastics may be used to fill in and make the whole habitable. Sheet metal and light metal castings afford a permanent material for the exteriors of such structures. Enclosures extremely light in weight combined with such structural elements relieve all modern building of surplus static; structure no longer an obesity or likely to fall of its own weight. Walls require little or no floor space. Spaces hitherto concealed or wasted or made impossible by heavy walls are revealed and made useful. Arrangements for human occupation in comfort may be so well aimed that spaciousness becomes economical as well as beautiful, appearing where it was never before thought to exist. Space now gives not only charm and character to practical occupation but beauty to the countenance and form of a valid new kind of habitation for mankind. Buildings, at long last — like their occupants — may be themselves free and wear the shining countenance of principle and directly say honestly, by free expression, yet becomingly, what they really are, what they really mean. The new sense of interior space as reality may characterize modern building. Style will be the consequence of integral character. Intellect thus reinforces and makes Spirit effective. An art as flexible, as various, as infinite in its possibilities as the spirit of man.

## ORGANIC UNIT

Thus environment and building are one: Planting the grounds around the building on the site as well as adorning the building take on new importance as they become features harmonious with the space-within-to-be-lived-in. Site, structure, furnishing — decoration too, planting as well — all these become as one in organic architecture. What was once called "decorating" — landscaping, lighting, etc. — and modern gadgetry (mechanical fixtures like air-conditioning) all are within the building structure as features of the building itself. Therefore all are elements of this synthesis of features of habitation and harmonious with environment. This is what *posterity* will call "modern architecture."

## VIII. SHELTER: INHERENT HUMAN FACTOR

EIGHT: As interior space to be lived in becomes the reality of building so shelter thus emphasized becomes more than ever significant in character and important as a feature. Shelter is still a strange disorder when reduced to a flat lid — though a common desire on account of economy. *To qualify this common-sense desire for shelter* as most significant feature of architecture is now in organic architecture of greatly increased importance. Witness, for instance: The new sense of spaciousness requires, as inherent human factor, significant cover as well as shade. Cover therefore now becomes in itself a feature more important as architectural form: Solidity of walls vanishing to reappear as imaginative screens involving light, and as inevitable consequence leaving more responsibility to the shapes and shaping of the whole building "overhead" with direct reference to the elements. Radical structural changes too now make the overhead lighter, less an imposition, more graceful, more harmonious feature of environment. Organic architecture sees shelter not only as a quality of space but of spirit, and the prime factor in any concept of building man into his environment as a legitimate feature of it. Weather is omnipresent and buildings must be left out in the rain. Shelter is dedicated to these elements. So much so that almost all other features of design tend to lead by one another to this important feature, shelter, and its component shade. In order to complete the building, protecting all within it from every changing circumstance of light, of cold and heat, of wear and tear and usage, we require shelter. The occupants of a building readily discover greater opportunity for comfort and more gracious, expanded living wherever shelter is becoming shade. By shade, charm has been added to character; style to comfort; significance to form.

## THE CLIENT

Thus modern architecture implies far more intelligent cooperation on the part of the client than ever before. New rewards being so much greater in a work of art than by any "good taste" of the usual client, the wisdom of human investment now lies in "the home as a work of art." Correspondingly, the architect becomes more important than ever. The dwelling "as-a-work-of-art" is a better place in which to be alive, to live with, and live for and by in every sense. Therefore, why not a better "investment"? The interests of architect and owner are thus mutual and binding upon both.

## IX. MATERIALS

NINE: I told my story of the nature of materials in building-construction in a series of articles written for Dr. Mikkelsen when he was editor of *The Architectural Record* of New York — about 1928. The good Doctor saved my economic life while I was getting a worm's eye view of society by calling me in to commission me to do a series of articles on "any subject I liked." I chose "The Nature of Materials," astonished to learn when starting research on the subject that nothing in any language had ever been written upon the subject.

All the materials usable in building-construction are more than ever important. They are all significant: each according to its own peculiar nature.

Old or new materials have their own lively contributions to make to the form, character and quality of any building. Each material may become a happy determinant of style; to use any one material wrongly is to abuse the integrity of the whole design.

## STYLE

There is no such thing as true style not indigenous. Let us now try to evaluate style. "Style *is* the man." Yes, style is, as should be, largely a matter of innate *character*. But style only becomes significant and impressive in architecture when it is thus integral or organic. Because it is innate it is style genuine — or not at all. Style is now a quality natural to the building itself. Style develops from *within*. Great repose — serenity, a new tranquility — is the reward for proper use of each or any material in the true forms of which each is naturally most capable.

## OWNERSHIP

In the hands of any prophetic architect the building is far more the owner's building than ever it was when built for him only by way of his, or her, own taste or whim. His building is the owner's now by his knowledge of the knowledge involved. So it is in the nature of architecture organic, that there can no longer be reason to deny any man his own way with his house if he really knows what he wants. The house may be designed to suit his preferences or his situation in his own way of life: but there is a difference between his preferences and his taste. If by his preferences, he reveals awareness of the principles involved and here touched upon, that will make his building genuinely his. If he seeks to understand *how* they involve, and evolve, his freedom *as individual* in this, his own, particular case his new home will declare his sovereignty as an enlightened individual. Homes of the new American *aristoi* may be as they must eventually become: one's own, not chiefly nor even ever "for sale." But this individual supremacy will come to the owner only with the knowledge of what it is that establishes this work of art as his own. "Taste" will now amount only to a certain discrimination in his approval of means to ends and appear once and for all in his choice of an architect. New light on both sides is indispensable to this new relationship, owner and architect.

Again, the *style* of each house may be much more than ever individual. Therefore the necessity for a new *cultural integrity* enters: individual sensitivity and personal responsibility are now essential. So comes a man-sized chance to choose a place not only in which to be alive, but in which to live as a distinguished entity, each individual owner genuinely a contributor to the indigenous culture of his time. Within the spirit of this wider range of individual choice, it becomes the home-owner's responsibility to be well aware of the nature of his choice of an architect. What he does now will not only surround him and represent him for life; it will probably be there for several hundred years. Integrity should appear in his life by his own choice. In our democracy the individual should rise to the higher level of aristocracy *only by his own perception of virtue*.

## WHAT IS NATURAL

As the consequence of these basic principles of design, wood and plaster will be content to be and will look as well as wood and plaster, will not aspire to be treated to resemble marble. Nor will concrete buildings, reinforced with steel, aim to resemble cut-stone or marble. Each will have a grammar of its own, true to materials, as in the new grammar of "Fallingwater", my first dwelling in reinforced concrete. Were this simple knowledge of the grammar, the syntax, of organic design to become actual performance, each building would show its nature with such honest distinction of form as a sentient architect might afford to the awakened, appreciative owner. Building is an organism only if in accord outside with inside and both with the character and nature of its purpose, process, place and time. It will then incorporate the nature of the site, of the methods by which it is constructed, and finally the whole — from grade to coping, ground to skyline — will be becoming to its purpose.

A lady does not wear diamonds to market nor appear in shorts in the hotel lobby. Why then should she live with disregard for parallel good sense in the conduct of her own home environment? Building as organism is now entitled to become a cultural asset.

This is all merely the common-sense of organic architecture.

## ADDENDUM I

New materials in construction and methods of good building slowly remake the aspect of the world. A new grammar of design in the use of materials, all capable of characteristic effects, should enrich the building of the world without overemphasis or ignorant abuse, should never become a cliché. However, not many such buildings are in evidence as thoroughbred.

## FURNITURE

Furnishings should be consistent in design and construction, and used with style as an extension in the sense of the building which they "furnish." Wherever possible all should be natural. The sure reward for maintaining these simple features of architectural integrity is great serenity. What makes this whole affair of house-building, furnishing and environment so difficult to come by is the fact that though a good sense of proportion, which is the breadth and essence of organic design, may find adequate response from good "taste," good taste is not a substitute for knowledge. A sense of proportion cannot be taught; a sense of proportion is born. Only so gifted can it be trusted as an affair of culture. Knowledge not only of the philosophy of building but its constitution is necessary. But there is no true understanding of any art without some knowledge of its philosophy. Only then does its meaning come clear.

## THE CAMERA EYE

If one would get the essential character of an organic building, it could not be by camera, inasmuch as it is wholly a matter of experience. One must be *in* the building before he can understand what makes it what it is. To write about it otherwise is false. Its pictorial aspects are purely incidental — but integral. Pictures of the buildings of the old two-dimensional school (nineteenth century) are most meaningful because they were seen as pictorial when conceived. But the building living before us now as an organism (twentieth century) may only be seen *by experience within* the actual structure. Since the depth-planes so characteristic of these structures are inevitable to their effects and are, chiefly, edgewise to the camera, any true sense of the whole edifice is seldom if ever found in a photograph. The depth-plane defies the flat camera-eye. Profoundly natural, these buildings are never dull or monotonous because this subtle quality of integrity due to "the each in each and the each in all" is continually there although not tangible to any superficial view. The essence of organic building is space, space flowing outward, space flowing inward (not necessarily by the use of the picture-window). Both plan and construction are seen to be inspired from within. For this important reason also, photographic views of these buildings are seldom satisfactory on the record. Only when the buildings are comprehended from within and each in its place a feature of its own special environment — serving its own appropriate purpose with integrity — are they really seen. If trees or mountains are round about, they will come to join and enrich the building by their natural sympathy. Architecture will become more charming because of this affinity. *The people in it gain the same distinction they would gain by being well-dressed.*

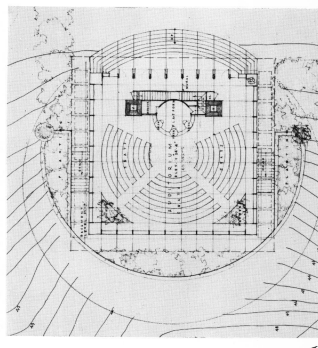

1957. CHRISTIAN SCIENCE CHURCH, BOLINAS, MARIN COUNTY, CALIFORNIA

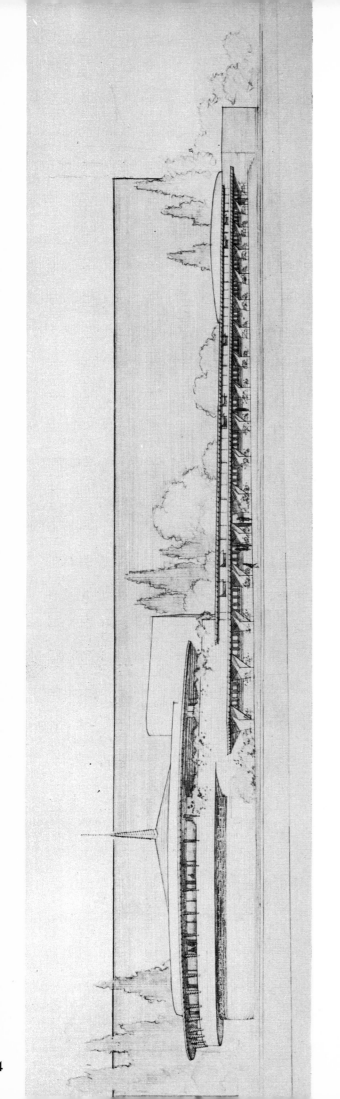

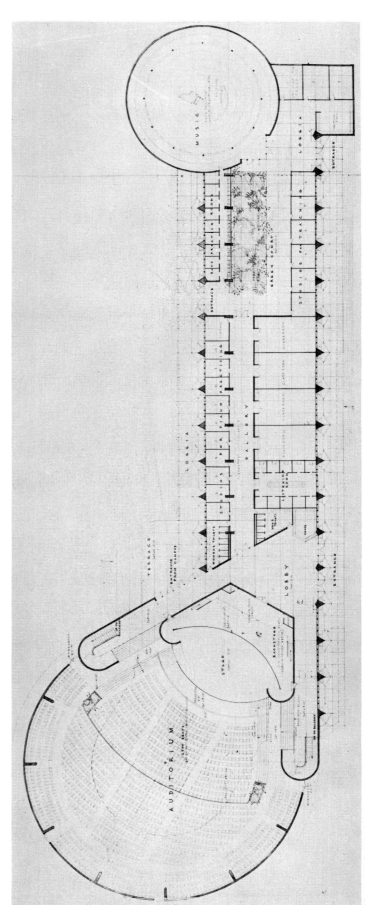

1957. MUSIC BUILDING, FLORIDA SOUTHERN COLLEGE, LAKELAND, FLORIDA, WITH PLAN OF LOWER FLOOR

UPPER PART OF
AUDITORIUM

ELEVATION AND PLAN OF BALCONY IN AUDITORIUM
MUSIC BUILDING FOR FLORIDA SOUTHERN COLLEGE
LAKELAND FLORIDA
FRANK LLOYD WRIGHT ARCHITECT

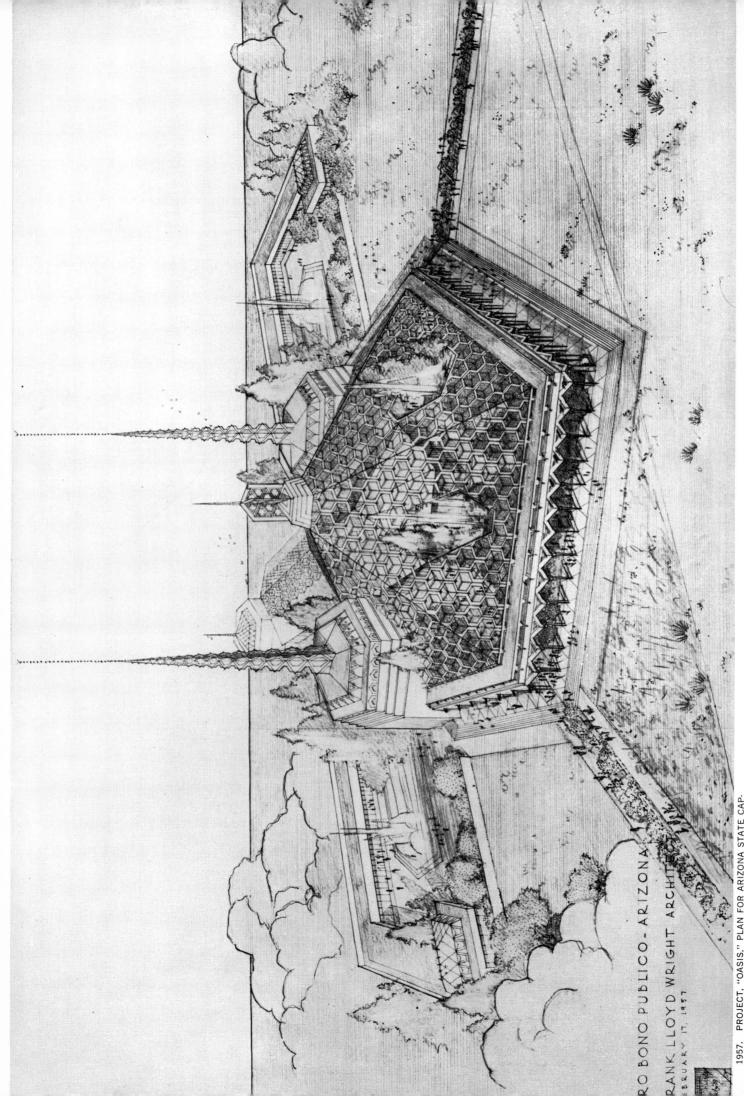

PRO BONO PUBLICO · ARIZONA

FRANK LLOYD WRIGHT ARCHITECT

FEBRUARY 17, 1957

1957.   PROJECT, "OASIS," PLAN FOR ARIZONA STATE CAP-
ITOL, PHOENIX, ARIZONA — PERSPECTIVE FROM THE AIR

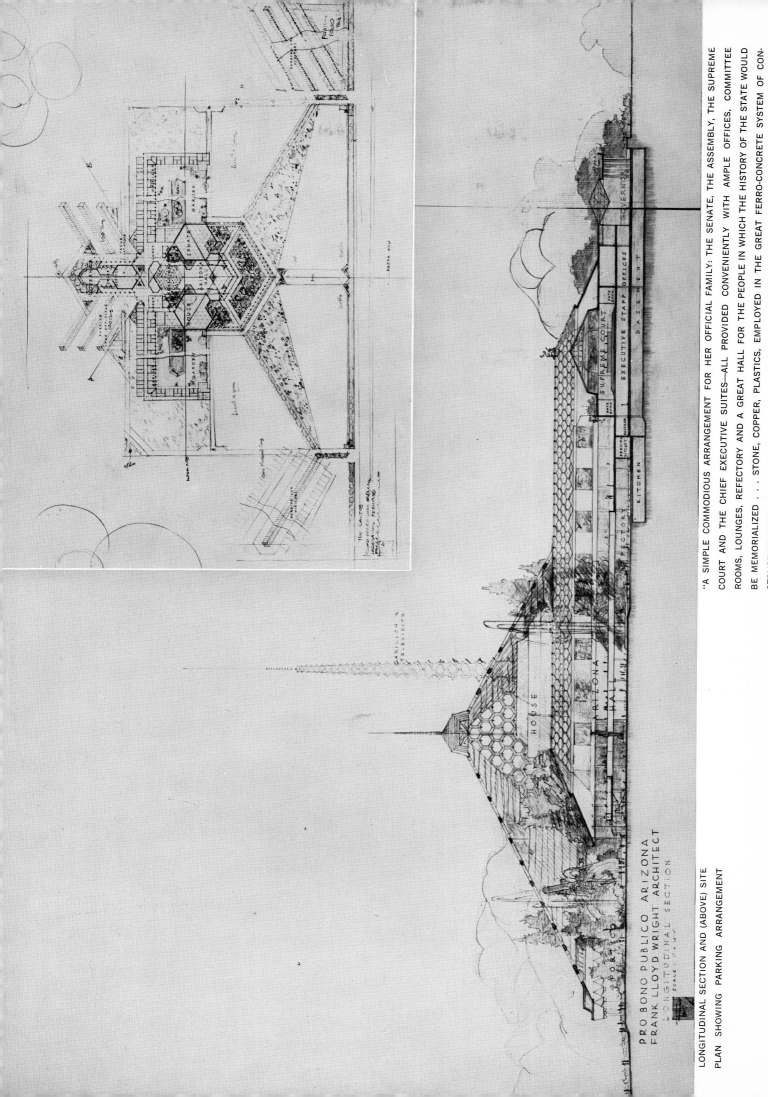

PRO BONO PUBLICO ARIZONA
FRANK LLOYD WRIGHT ARCHITECT
LONGITUDINAL SECTION
SCALE 1" = 40'

LONGITUDINAL SECTION AND (ABOVE) SITE
PLAN SHOWING PARKING ARRANGEMENT

"A SIMPLE COMMODIOUS ARRANGEMENT FOR HER OFFICIAL FAMILY: THE SENATE, THE ASSEMBLY, THE SUPREME
COURT AND THE CHIEF EXECUTIVE SUITES—ALL PROVIDED CONVENIENTLY WITH AMPLE OFFICES, COMMITTEE
ROOMS, LOUNGES, REFECTORY AND A GREAT HALL FOR THE PEOPLE IN WHICH THE HISTORY OF THE STATE WOULD
BE MEMORIALIZED . . . STONE, COPPER, PLASTICS, EMPLOYED IN THE GREAT FERRO-CONCRETE SYSTEM OF CON-
STRUCTION THAT NOW CONSTITUTES THE TWENTIETH CENTURY BODY OF OUR WORLD."

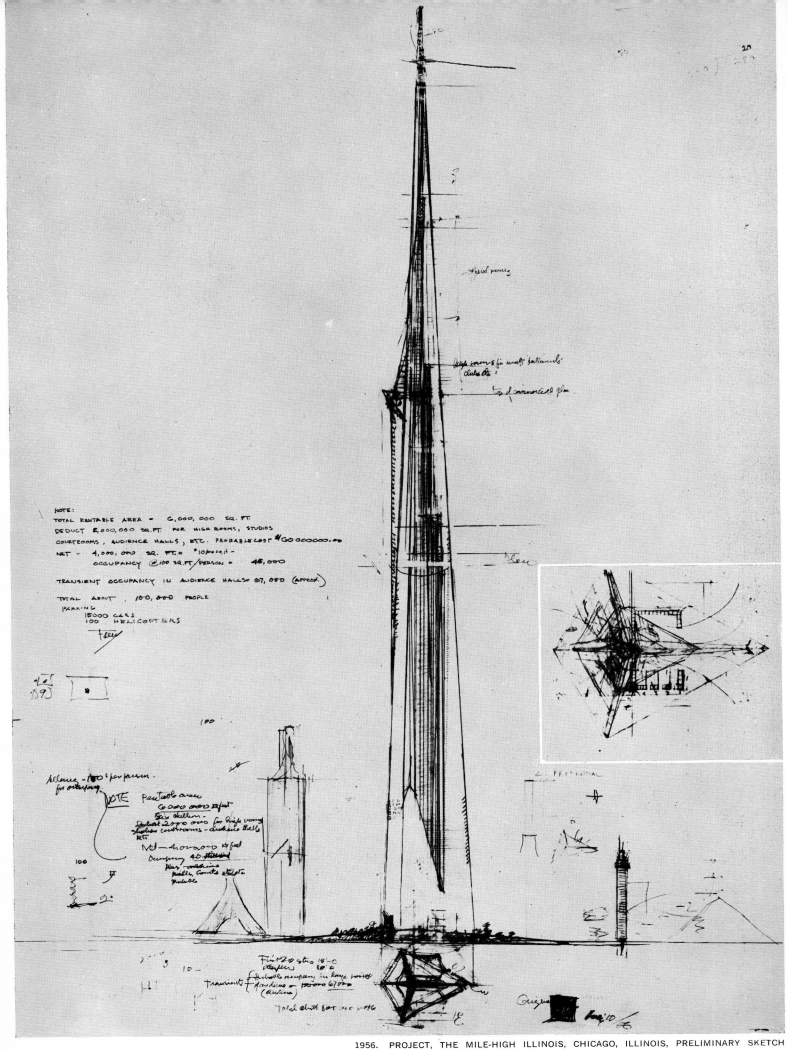

1956. PROJECT, THE MILE-HIGH ILLINOIS, CHICAGO, ILLINOIS, PRELIMINARY SKETCH

# THE MILE-HIGH ILLINOIS

CANTILEVER SKY-CITY · 528 STORIES · TRIPOD IN PLAN · ONE MILE HIGH FROM GRADE TO TOP FLOOR, DIVIDED INTO FOUR SECTIONS · EXPOSED MEMBERS ALUMINUM OR STAINLESS STEEL · ELEVATORS ESPECIALLY DESIGNED TANDEM-CABS RATCHET-GUIDED TYPE, ATOMIC POWER · ESCALATOR SERVICE BASEMENTS AND FIRST FIVE FLOORS · FOUR QUADRUPLE-LANE APPROACHES TO EACH OF THE FOUR ENTRANCES · ONE ENTRANCE AT EACH CORNER · PARKING FOR ABOUT 15,000 CARS AND LANDING DECKS FOR 150 HELICOPTERS

## SPECIFICATION

1. Of all forms of upright structure, most stable is the tripod: pressures upon any side immediately resisted by the other two. For general stability at great height this form of the ILLINOIS is planned to employ the new principles of cantilever—steel in suspension—as in the Imperial Hotel, Tokyo, the Johnson Heliolaboratory at Racine, Wisconsin, and Price Tower at Bartlesville, Oklahoma. The exterior of the ILLINOIS is entirely metal. The exterior wall screens are suspended from the edges of the rigid upright steel cores—cores buried in light-weight concrete: this building thus designed from the inside outward instead of the dated steel-framed construction from outside inward. The entire structure is thus more airplane in character (twentieth century construction) than the usual heavy nineteenth century building. For instance, the support of the outer walls and sixteen feet of the outer area of the floors is pendent, and the science of continuity is employed everywhere else. From inside outward always. Floor-slabs are extended across the vertical central core. All floor-loads are balanced against each other over central supports, even the outer perimeter of floor slabs and exterior walls which are suspended from the cores. The science of continuity thus employs the type of construction similar to that of the airplane and ocean liner. The Imperial Hotel and the Price Tower, the National Life Insurance Building, the Johnson Heliolaboratory, Fallingwater, etc. were all of this type of structure: a "natural" for either great spans or great heights. Throughout the ILLINOIS typical weights of this structure are little more than half those of nineteenth century building practice: the customary bridge-engineers' welded steel framing.

2. This interior system of building-construction is new: twentieth century. Tension as here involved in the ILLINOIS (upright) was first used by myself in the Imperial Hotel (horizontally), 1915, and proved earthquake-proof, 1922. The same general system has now been repeated vertically—and successfully—in the nineteen story, forty-foot square, Price Tower—steel-in-tension there used as years before in the Heliolaboratory.

The same principle centralizes loads over a giant core of properly designed steel fabrication in the ILLINOIS, cast in appropriate masses of light-weight concrete. As all floor loads balance each other over staunch rigid cores, with the outer portion of the slabs and the outer wall-screens suspended from these cores, the framework of the ILLINOIS is like a tree—the horizontal floor slabs integral with the vertical cores, making the total structure light and rigid, not rickety.

3. The 528 light floor slabs are hollow, tapered from the cores to carry air-conditioning, lighting and appurtenance systems. These cantilevered floor slabs are formed by special high-tension steel, diamond-mesh reinforced, and cast into light concrete slabs. Excepting vertical elevator enclosures, which issue from the sloping sides of the tripod, all exterior surface-features of this structure and certain outer areas of the floors also are suspended by steel strands from the sloping corners of the core as already described. Outer glass surfaces are set four feet back under the metal parapets to avoid glare of glass and afford a human sense of protection at such enormous heights as characterize the ILLINOIS SKY-CITY.

4. Elevator transit is by atomic power; especially designed elevators, each five stories high, serving in series the five divisions of 100-floor heights. A group of 76 tandem-cab elevators five units high begin to load where the escalators leave off at the fifth floor. These elevators entirely independent of ordinary suspension systems. As motorized they rise and emerge on ratchet-guides, soaring into the air, independent of, yet an integral feature of the tripod, and appear outside the tripod as graceful vertical features of the ILLINOIS. The entire elevator system thus rises perfectly upright to five different story-heights. Special through-service is provided to the upper stories and to the very top floor at various speeds all the way to one mile above the ground floor level. All elevators are motivated by atomic power, engines on the cabs engaging ratchet-tracks, cabs moving vertically at various speeds much as

an automobile runs on the level. Approximate speed: say, a mile per minute; appropriate automatic stop-and-go controls without attendance are to be provided. Additional private lifts may connect various departments independently of main elevators. Cars are set aside for non-stop emergency service. As escalators from the lower parking levels serve the first five stories, the main floor of the ILLINOIS is thus practically the fifth floor. This combination escalator-elevator service should empty the entire building within the hour by day and the various occupations by night in half the time.

5. The ILLINOIS employs the now proved system of "tap-root" foundation sloping to hard-pan or bed-rock, again similar to the foundations of the Helio-laboratory and the Price Tower; all similar in principle to the foundation system that saved the structure of the Imperial Hotel in the 1922 temblor. To make rigidity possible at the extreme heights of the ILLINOIS, this type of foundation continues the main core into the ground to reach rock or hard-pan formation beneath. The foundation has available spaces within it for utilities, owing to its tapered form. Final drilling into bedrock for insert of the spinal cores is not difficult to construct.

6. Finally—throughout this light-weight tensilized structure, because of the integral character of all members, loads are in equilibrium at all points,

doing away with oscillation. There would be no sway at the peak of the ILLINOIS.

A rapier, with handle the breadth of the hand, set firmly into the ground, blade upright, as a simile, indicates the general idea of the ILLINOIS five times the height of the highest structure in the world.

7. Exterior features: the elevators, outer parapets, all exposed horizontal or vertical members are of gold-colored metal and, with the windows set back under steel parapets to avoid glare, give the building emphasis as an all metal structure.

8. Covered parking for about 15,000 cars may be reached by ramps connected to one central level below grade and four levels above. These lower levels and the sub-floor parking beneath the building itself have direct access to and from escalators; there above, beside the main building, are two decks, each for 75 helicopters.

IN GENERAL: The ILLINOIS is divided into four parts, and is reached at four points by four four-lane approaches. Fountain features and green-planted parterres are thus related to the tripod entrances, each independent of the other.

The riveted or welded steel framing of the nineteenth century has been abandoned. All this well done, this great twentieth-century edifice will be more permanent than the Pyramids.

| AREAS OF THE ILLINOIS | GROSS AREA | NET RENTABLE AREA |
|---|---|---|
| From Grade level to entrance level | 490,000 sq. ft. | 374,000 sq. ft. |
| Entrance level to 1st elevator floor | 480,000 sq. ft. | 364,000 sq. ft. |
| 1st elevator floor to 110th floor | 8,050,000 sq. ft. | 5,250,000 sq. ft. |
| 111th floor to 328th floor | 7,800,000 sq. ft. | 5,840,000 sq. ft. |
| 329th floor to 428th floor | 1,150,000 sq. ft. | 850,000 sq. ft. |
| 429th floor to 528th floor | 492,000 sq. ft. | 369,000 sq. ft. |
| T O T A L S | 18,462,000 sq. ft. | 13,047,000 sq. ft. |

IN SPACIOUS COMFORT APPROXIMATE TOTAL POPULATION 130,000 INHABITANTS

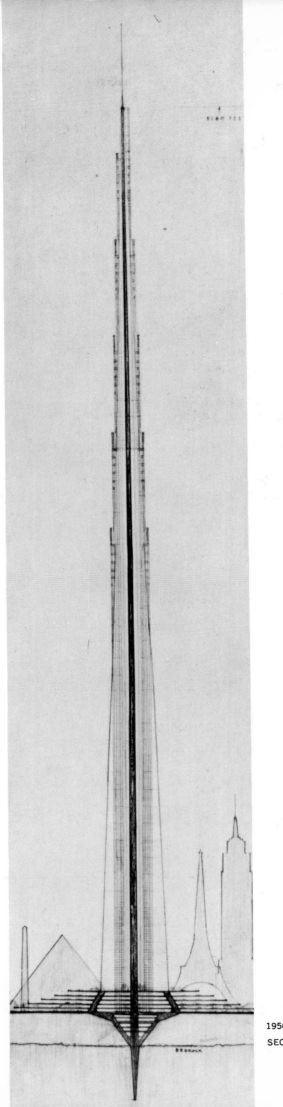

1956.  PROJECT, THE MILE-HIGH ILLINOIS, CHICAGO, ILLINOIS
SECTION SHOWING TAPROOT FOUNDATION IN BEDROCK

if truth becomes the chief concern of our serious citizens and their artists, architects and men of religion, independent of established authority?

## THEY ALSO SERVE

Nevertheless I realize that if all false or unfriendly forces (due to ignorance or so conditioned as here described) inimical to culture, were to become less and less, many long years would still be needed to overcome the deep habituations that have been built into the American scene by inroads upon the American character; wholly against natural grain and against our glorious original aim. If this twentieth century architecture, true to the principles of construction and more in line with our democratic faith, were to be more widely acknowledged by established authority; even if it were to be proclaimed from the housetops by cinema, television, press, politics, government and society as "the right thing" to be studied and practiced — there would still be controversy. Controversy would, even then, continue for the coming half-century at least, would perhaps never cease. Democracy knows only too well the senseless weight and conflicts of irresponsible public opinion, the chronic oralism, the dead weight of ignorance, the prejudices of conditioned minds siding right or left with selfish interests of hearts hardened — instead of the deep faith in Man necessary to inspire enlightenment by generosity of motive, which democracy meant to our forefathers and must yet mean to us. The common sense of the simple truth in this new-old philosophy, *from within outward,* if awakened in our society as now in our architecture, would ensure the true uses of technology for human shelter and reverential harmonious environment, both socially and politically. It would soon get into politics.

Meanwhile we continue to hope that the Comic Spirit in which we as a people do excel may survive long enough to salt and savor life among us long enough for our civilization to present us to the world as a culture, not merely as an amazing civilization. The basic distinction between the curious and the beautiful, in which culture really consists, will make all the difference between a society with a creative soul and a society with none.

PART TWO

work of manhood. This inner light as it shines that loves architecture, art and Religion are ever-so symbolic ... Again we may call it humane ... such as it is that men take their charm ... two or three men here in this school of hers ...

## HUMANITY—THE LIGHT OF THE WORLD

Constantly I have referred to a more "humane" architecture, so I will try to explain what *humane* means to me, an architect. Like organic architecture, the quality of humanity is *interior* to man. As the solar system is reckoned in terms of light-years, so may the inner light be what we are calling humanity. This element, Man as light, is beyond all reckoning. Buddha was known as the light of Asia; Jesus as the light of the world. Sunlight is to nature as this interior *light* is to man's spirit: Manlight.

Manlight is above instinct. Human imagination by way of this interior light is born, conceives, creates: dies but to continue the light of existence only as this light lived in the man. The spirit is illumined by it and to the extent that his life *is* this light and it proceeds from him, it in turn illumines his kind. Affirmations of this light in human life and work are man's true happiness.

There is nothing higher in human consciousness than beams of this interior light. We call them beauty. Beauty is but the shining of man's light — radiance the high romance of his manhood as we know Architecture, the Arts, Philosophy, Religion, to be romantic. All come to nourish or be nourished by this inextinguishable light within the soul of man. He can give no intellectual consideration above or beyond this inspiration. From the cradle to the grave his true being craves this reality to assure the continuation of his life as Light thereafter.

As sunlight falls around a helpless thing, revealing form and countenance, so a corresponding light, of which the sun is a symbol, shines from the inspired work of mankind. This inner light is assurance that man's Architecture, Art and Religion, are as one — its symbolic emblems. Then we may call *humanity* itself the light that never fails. Baser elements in man are subject to this miracle of his own light. Sunrise and sunset are appropriate symbols of man's existence on earth.

There is no more precious element of immortality than mankind as thus humane. Heaven may be the symbol of this light of lights only insofar as heaven is thus a haven.

Mankind has various names for this interior light, "the soul" for instance. To be truly *humane* is divinity in the only sense conceivable. There can be no such thing as absolute death or utter evil — all being from light in some form. In any last analysis there is no evil because shadow itself is of the light.

And so when Jesus said "the kingdom of God is within you," I believe this is what he meant. But his disciples betrayed his meaning when they removed the Father, supreme light, from the human heart to inhabit a realm of his own, because it was too difficult for human beings to find faith in man. So Christianity, itself misled, put out the interior light in order to organize worship of life as exterior light. Man is now too subject to his intellect instead of true to his own spirit. Whenever this inner light of the man has been submerged in the darkness of discord and failure he has invented "Satan" to explain the shadow. Insofar as light becomes thus inorganic, humanity will never discover the unity of mankind. Only by interior light is this possible. Science seems to be going toward the physical discovery that light is the essence of human being so far as life itself can be known.

Genesis: "Let there be light and there was light."

"More light," said the dying Goethe and he, no doubt, found it.

Then let this rediscovery of Architecture as Man and Man as Architecture illumine the edifice in every feature and shine forth as the countenance of truth. The freedom of his art will thus find consecration in the soul of man.

# AMERICAN GENIUS

So the genius of our democracy still lies hidden in the eternal law of change: Growth, our best hope, consists in understanding at last what other civilizations have only known about and left to us — ourselves comforted meantime by the realization that all one does either for or against Truth serves it equally well.


FRANK LLOYD WRIGHT
Taliesin

# PHOTOGRAPHERS' CREDITS

P. E. GUERRERO:   Frontispiece (courtesy House and Garden), 168, 175

HEDRICH-BLESSING:   165

HOLLAND:   167 (bottom)

W. ALBERT MARTIN:   144

MAYNARD L. PARKER:   69, 70, 71, 72, 193, 194, 195, 198, 199, 200
        (courtesy House Beautiful)

JOE D. PRICE:   197

AARON SISKIND AND RICHARD NICKEL:   78, 79
        (courtesy Architectural Forum)

EZRA STOLLER:   166

H. S. K. YAMAGUCHI:   124, 125